BRIANA COLLINS

# MIRROR IMAGE

A BOOK ABOUT IDENTITY, FREEDOM, AND JESUS

# TABLE OF CONTENTS

# INTRODUCTION

One of the top trending issues in today's church culture is identity. The pursuit of identity and the typical companion pursuit of freedom are widely accepted as noble pursuits. But all too often, what begins as a noble goal can result in the making of an idol. If we are to seek first His Kingdom and His righteousness, then even our search for identity and freedom must first begin with who Jesus is and His righteousness. You can pursue identity and freedom and you will gain some, but if you pursue Jesus even above these things, you will find everything.

Too many well-intentioned believers have found themselves in a vicious cycle of looking inward not only to diagnose their personal struggles, but also to find their solutions. I've seen believers set themselves on a journey of self-discovery only to find that the path is riddled with self-centric distractions that limit their ability to see beyond their shortcomings and even blinded by their own strengths. The idea that we can identify ourselves and therefore create personas that we can manipulate and control in order to become the best version of ourselves will still only leave us with what we can do on our own and, without realizing it, apart from God. The need for identity never seems to be met because the pursuit of our identity has felt more powerful and enticing than even the pursuit of Christ.

I've watched so many Christians become so enamored by the promise of freedom, that the pursuit of freedom became more alluring to them than the prize of the Presence of the God where freedom actually resides. Similarly to a runner's high, the excitement of the accomplishment becomes the motivation to keep coming back to the same place. Unknowingly, the freedom with which they were given that was meant to be shared to free others, became the "hit" that kept them perpetually focused on self. When this happens, the well will run dry, and they will have to find ways to keep filling that well on their own. Freedom will then become a string of isolated events instead of a deep well of living water to drink from and serve to others.

If we find our identity and freedom in Christ, we will find the endless well of Living Water. You can search for a cup of water and eventually be left with an empty cup, or you could search for the well that is constantly being sourced by the River of Life and never run out. It's as simple as your source. You can be your own source and be confined to your own limitations, or you could live from the Source of Life and be constantly filled to overflowing. Finding your identity and living in the freedom that Jesus paid for you to have are both important elements of your inheritance as a Child of God. Your heavenly Father wants you to live abundantly in both. But, what if there is a better way than we've known to look at identity and freedom?

What if we have been looking in a mirror to find our image, when we should be looking to see the image of our Savior? And the mirror we thought we needed is obsolete because as we look deeper into the eyes of Jesus, we find that we are meant to be a mirror that reflects Him. What if you are His mirror image?

This book is about identity and freedom, but those cannot be found without first finding Jesus. So, we are going to break the cycles of the inferior goal of finding our own identity and instead we are going to dive deep into the superior goal of finding the identity of Christ. This book is actually about revelations of the identity of Jesus. My prayer is that, as you read this book, God will reveal to you the identity of Jesus and the freedom He shares with you in a deeper intimacy than you have ever known. My hope is that you would read this book alongside Him, and that you will see Jesus in a new way. My prayer is that you will encounter Christ and find healing in your

———

As Christ Himself is seen for *who He really is*, who you really are will also be revealed.

———

mind, soul, and body. I believe you will find freedom in the embrace of Jesus and with that same freedom, you will bring freedom to those around you. I believe that as a result of pursuing the identity of Jesus that you will live a life more aware of and engaged in His Presence and His identity. And in turn, you will know how He sees you and the life He died for you to live. Let's begin this journey with scripture as it will set the tone for the rest of this book and what I hope to be just the beginning of your beautiful pursuit of the identity of Jesus.

> Christ's resurrection is your resurrection too. This is why we are to yearn for all that is above for that's where Christ sits enthroned at the place of all power, honor, and authority! Yes, feast on all the treasures of the heavenly realm and fill your thoughts with heavenly realities, and not with the distractions of the natural realm. Your crucifixion with Christ has severed the tie to this life, and now your true life is hidden away in God in Christ. And as Christ himself is seen for who he really is, who you really are will also be revealed, for you are now one with him in his glory! Colossians 3:1-4 (TPT)

As Christ Himself is seen for who He really is, who you really are will also be revealed.

You are His mirror image.

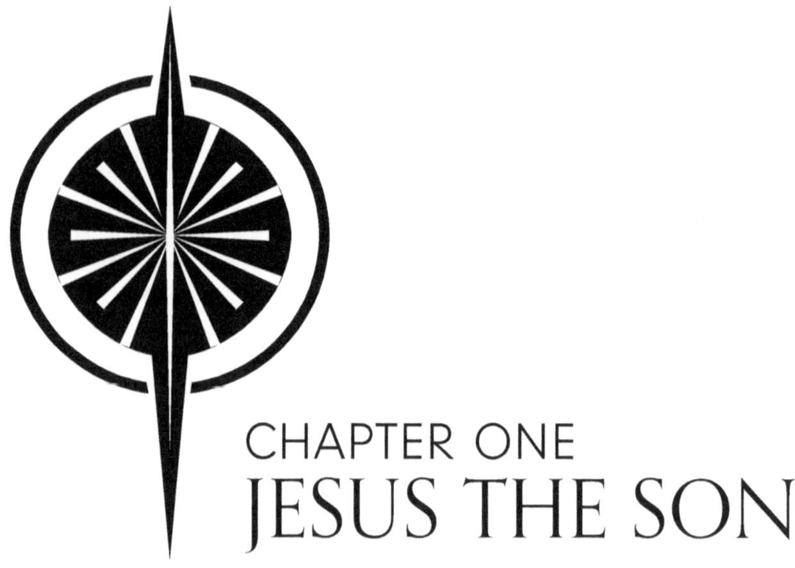

# CHAPTER ONE
# JESUS THE SON

Identity. The great pursuit of our day. The supposed key that unlocks the meaning to why we exist and how we ought to live our lives. This presumably noble quest has been shrouded in a belief system that has driven us to create our own mirrors by which we strive to find a glimpse of identity. These mirrors are framed by good intentions, but our efforts have led us to exchange what was meant to be a reflection of the eternal for a confined image of what is temporal. Without realizing the cost of the mirrors, we have traded the only identity we were ever meant to pursue for an image of our own understanding. Our own reflections are images that can be anticipated, limited, and even manipulated to fit a desired look. Pursuing our own image feels like a manageable endeavor and can even be considered a channel to find a sense of control.

In essence, the search for identity, even among believers, has survived on the idea that we could be our own god. We abandoned the only pursuit we were designed to embark on for our own sense of control. This search for identity has led us to man-made constructs that, at best, open our eyes to formulas that produce merely good habits, and at worst, blind us to the only pursuit that would fulfill us.

This blindness has rendered far too many believers fruitless in their own lives and absent from a world that desperately needs us to reflect the image of the Son.  We were never meant to build our own mirror. We were the ones who were lost, not the One who would find. We have been found in Christ yet still distracted with the pursuit of ourselves. To set out on this inferior search requires the subtle belief of lingering separation between the Father and His children. We need a revelation of identity, but not our own. We need a revelation of Jesus. This book will be a journey through revelations of the identity of Christ through Scripture and will awaken you to the reality that you have been born again to live in, here and now .

So, what is our reality, here and now? We have to cut away the distractions that are vying for our attention and begging for our agreement that truth is fluid. There is only one truth. And that truth would have to be Truth Himself, Jesus. All things began in Him, all things exist in Him, and all things return to Him. He is the beginning and the end. It was by Him that we exist as we were spoken into creation by His voice. The Word Himself, Jesus. It may seem cliché to say the answer is always, Jesus. But it is the simple truth. And it's the truth that sets us free.

But sets us free from what? As believers, we can all say what we've been saved from. We've been saved from eternal separation from God. We've been saved from hell. But are we meant to live here and now, focused only on what we've been saved from?

I don't believe so.

I believe that we are to become more aware and more focused on what we've been saved into, the kingdom of heaven, here and now. Jesus said, "Seek first the kingdom of heaven and all its righteousness." The answer is not to escape the world, to try really hard at being good, or to endure a miserable life until you die and get to heaven. Jesus came so that we may have life and have it more abundantly. That life does not begin when our physical bodies die. It begins the moment we are crucified with Christ in His death and are raised in the life of Jesus in our spirits. Jesus came to bring us back to Him. Jesus came to bring His presence. And in His Presence is where we find the life He died for us to live.

If we live our lives with the perspective of only having escaped hell, we'll live

Jesus came to bring us back to Him. Jesus came to bring His presence. And in *His Presence* is where we find the life He died for us to live.

as barely scraping by in a world that we view as doomed, instead of living
as a citizen of heaven who are here to bring our reality in the kingdom of
heaven to a world that Jesus lived and died to reconcile to Himself. Our hope
is not confined to only the future, but our hope is anchored in the One in
whom time exists. A hope that covers the past, moves in the present, and
has already gone into the future. This is not a hope that looks to the future
to be truly free, rather the actual hope of the truth that Jesus did go down
to hell and He did take back the keys, and that He rose.  And when He rose,
He carried with Him all salvation. He ascended to Heaven to sit at the right
hand of the Father. Jesus spent eternity in heaven before coming to earth. He
was slain before the foundations of the world, and so His rescue plan was
always to come from heaven to earth because without Him, there was no
way to get from earth to heaven. If that is His perspective, that He would
bring heaven to earth, then that should be our perspective as well. We are
meant to look at everything we see on earth, including ourselves, with a lens
that gives preeminence to the reality of heaven.. But so often we have an Old
Testament perspective of from earth to heaven. We view heaven as where we
go eventually, as opposed to heaven being the very place that we are seated
in, here and now.

The Pharisees were experts in the "from earth to heaven perspective."
To them, everything was about lifeless rules and formulas for achieving
godliness. They assumed that heaven could be achieved through innocence.
I want to take a second to clarify this point. According to the law of Moses,
if every law was carefully observed and every sin properly atoned for, that
acceptance could be given to those who faithfully complied. When Jesus
came, He taught that entering the kingdom of heaven would require more
than following rules to get from earth to heaven. Instead, heaven would have
to come to them.

But, for those who believed that they could only enter the kingdom of
heaven based on their own works and efforts, they created a self-centric
ideology that kept them isolated and distracted from the truth that was right
in front of them. Many of the Pharisees and Sadducees refused to believe in
Jesus as the Son of God and continued to wrestle their way through life by
their own earthly merits and self-righteousness. So, why would those of us
who have believed in Jesus as the Son of God and who have been born again
as a child of God, still live with a life philosophy so similar to a law that we

were released form the curse of and that which has already been fulfilled by Jesus? Are we relying on our own efforts and our own self-righteousness? Do we feel confined by the limitations of our own efforts and the reality of a broken world? Or are we living in the reality of heaven on earth?

All through our lives, God wants to take us from glory to glory. But if we assume a reality that is incongruent with who we really are in Christ, then we will never understand why we're here and we'll never see the reality that we are meant to live in here and now. All too often, children of God spend their lives spinning their wheels trying to attain what has already been given to them in Christ.

I was very rules-oriented as a child. I liked to be in control. And seeing rules as something to manipulate and navigate helped me feel like I could control my life. The need to feel in control is what drives so many of us, actually, all of us, to live lives that make ourselves our source. And the truth is, control, as God intended it, is not a bad thing. Self-control is a fruit of the Spirit. The belief that we must fight for control over our own lives  already starts us down a dangerous path because we will only fight for what we believe is not already ours or what we believe is being taken away from us. Inside each of us has been instilled a sense and an ability to make choices. God hard-wired humanity for free will. Biblical self-control requires a Spirit-led life. It requires that we lay down our lives to submit to the Lordship of Jesus. And within that surrender, we acknowledge our responsibility to use the power of free will, willingly laying down our version of a limited self-god and moving in the infinite possibilities with God. Self-control, the way that God intends it to be, is choosing to partner with God and obey Him. But control, as a self-preservation method, will always lead you to being your own source, trying to control your world in your own power. This counterfeit will require you to manipulate situations and oftentimes, other people. This system sets you as the center of your world. And it leads you to loneliness. It leads you to disconnection.

As a child, one of the aspects of my life that I felt securely in control of was school. I really liked to get straight A's and to acquire as much information as possible. As they say, "knowledge is power" and it felt that way to me even at a young age. I achieved accolades like spelling bee trophies and honor roll certificates. I was very performance-driven, and that creeped into my relationship with God. It was as if the Bible had become a textbook for me. I could figure this thing out on my own. I could make this work for me. I felt like I was in control. And before I could even realize what was happening, I turned my relationship with God into a religion.

I was extremely formula-focused. I really thought that the Christian life was just one big formula with a bunch of subsequent formulas to get what you want and maintain control of your life. I chose processes, formulas, and rules, and I called that faith. And this pattern seemed to work for me because I felt like I could check off all the boxes of and maintain control of my "report card" in Christian life.

I remember a time in my early twenties being so convinced that I had mastered the science of formula-led Christianity that I could hardly withstand the blow when my paradigm of control was finally exposed to be fragile illusion. My husband and I hadn't been married for very long before we began experiencing some hard times financially. Right around the time our first daughter was born, we had made the naïve decision to invest money we didn't have in a short-term investment that promised a large and fast return. So, we pulled cash advances from all of our credit cards and secured a very large line of credit to finance this lofty endeavor. As we waited for our money and profit to come, it became clear that something had gone wrong. We just happened to come into this little investment group at the very tipping point of a Ponzi scheme that had finally caught up with the owner. Not only were we out $40,000, but that money was all from credit. We were left with minimum payments we couldn't keep up with and interest of an additional $2000/month being accrued. To say we were in over our heads was an understatement.

As the fear and anxiety rose with every bill, I started to crash. My parents were trying their best to help me walk through the emotions of stress and anxiety and flat-out frustration. I was already well past my last nerve even before the heated conversation started because I was so tired of the fight with our finances, and all my parents could offer me were things that I already knew. And as most young adults will attest to, there are few things more aggravating than being told what to do when you think you already know everything. So, as the three of us stood in the kitchen and the conversation became more intense, through tears and a lot of anger I just yelled out! "I know! I know all the formulas! I know how to fix this."

I had reduced God in my heart to a distant teacher and elevated myself to the savior of my circumstances. I thought that If I would just quote all the right Bible verses, demanded every declaration of prosperity, denied the problems existence according to my faulty understanding of faith, and followed the rules to a successful life, that I could manipulate and control a system designed for me to get what I want. I would have never considered this to be wrong at the time because I thought that God had devised a list of biblical formulas and then left us to study hard enough to get the right answers and pass the test. I thought this was the life of faith He wanted me to live. I thought my strength pleased Him. I didn't realize that God was not going after my behavior or waiting for me to pass some sort of life test, He was going after my heart. He wanted to meet me in the mess to lead me out of it, but I thought He wanted me to save myself.

Hearing God's voice and recognizing His presence were the last things on my mind. And I was miserable. I had reduced my relationship with God to a formula of attaining what I thought I needed. I was convinced that the answer I was seeking was financial stability. I thought the answer to a financial crisis was more money. I was convinced that I needed to manufacture the product of an equation based on formulas that I called faith and confessions.  Somewhere along the line, I believed this to be my savior. And with this theology, I brought myself to a place where I believed in a God whose Presence wasn't necessary. I believed I could save us from this financial misery on my own terms, and I used the Bible as my validation to do so. I wanted to extract scripture and determine its theology based on my need, rather than the truth that all scripture is meant to point to Christ. I didn't need more money. I needed Jesus. But, my lack of money exposed my dependence on it. My desire for money to be the answer, exposed where I had opened my heart to a savior other than Jesus.

My supposed textbook, the Bible, was sure to have a definitive answer for me. In the human quest to take and maintain control of our lives, many Christians have looked at the Bible as an answer key. The Bible has been mistaken for a neatly packaged guide with a beginning, middle, and end. Easily memorized and even more easily quoted. Available to us to pick apart, dissect, and manipulate to achieve our desired outcomes. Our ticket to use

———

Trust is
*our response*
to the identity
of God.

———

at our disposal and bend to our control, rather than an invitation to peer past the pages into One who is both the Beginning and the End and yet He is eternal. The Bible is meant to engage us in a conversation with Jesus, who is the Word.

In my arrogance, I looked to what I thought had been left to me to succeed in life, without further need of His Presence. I just wanted the formula to plug my particular factors into, to create a solution that would save us. I was convinced I needed to produce a savior. A savior that would pull us out of financial despair and into financial abundance. I was positive this was what God wanted for me. That He had left me with formulas to create the products of prayer that I sought. I was convinced I needed to be saved financially, and if it was money that was the problem, then it would be money that would save me.

We can say things that sound so Christian-like. I can't tell you how many times I've heard a Christian, including myself, say, "I am really trusting God for my finances." Translation - I am in debt up to my eyeballs and I need money to get myself out of this. Money from God of course, but nonetheless, what I need is money.

If we are trusting God for our finances only when we are experiencing financial hardships, then who are we trusting for our finances when our bank accounts are full? I've only ever heard someone say they are trusting God for their finances when their finances are a mess. I've never heard someone say this when in a time of financial abundance

The idea that we somehow have to adjust our faith levels according to our finances will set us up for an extremely limited mindset. This belief will tell us that you only need to trust God for provision until you make enough money that you aren't concerned about it anymore. Once you are out of the financial hardship, you can go back to being the one you rely on instead of God. And it empowers a subtle belief within that says, money is my savior. Faith is never meant to be a reaction to the problem. Faith is meant to be our response to God. If our faith is dependent on our needs, this sets a tone for us that leads us to circumvent our need for God in our finances, and any other aspect of our lives, to chase after the presence of the answer and outcomes we seek rather than the presence of God. It's like telling God, thanks for bringing me out of hell. I'll call you if I need you again. I have your manual on how to live a successful life, And when I need to trust you because my circumstances tell me to, I will.

Our trust levels should not be based on our needs. Our trust in God should always be based on who He is. Trust is a byproduct of relationship. Trust is our response to the identity of God.

In the Message translation, in John 8, Jesus answers the Pharisees' plea to give them more than just His word that He is the Messiah, and Jesus says this:

> You're right that you only have my word. But you can depend on it being true. I know where I've come from and where I go next. You don't know where I've come from and where I go next. You don't know where I'm from or where I'm headed. You decide according to what you can see and touch. I don't make judgments like that. But even if I did, my judgment would be true because I wouldn't make it out of the narrowness of my experience but in the largeness of the One who sent me, the Father.

Jesus did not form his understanding of reality out of earth's experiences, but rather in the Presence of the Father.

I was trusting in myself to "get it right" and achieve the status of financial freedom I desired. I had become my own source and didn't even realize it. I trusted myself and viewed Biblical knowledge as my tools. To me, the Bible was a list of to-dos and not to-dos. And I felt secure in my process, not in my God! I, unknowingly, lived as if He wasn't even part of the equation. As if He had set this process up and walked away. I had faith in faith, faith in myself to get it right. I saw myself as left here on earth by God with a textbook full of formulas to work it out on my own. From the perspective of "from earth to heaven," I had what I needed to toil my way through life until I finally got to heaven, where I could finally be set free. The whole point is getting from earth to heaven, right? Isn't that why we were saved? To escape hell? To eventually be in heaven?

Acting as my own source, I was trying to control and manipulate the hand of God in my life. But, God is not a genie in a lamp. He's our Father. I had the life of the Almighty God inside of me, and I was still missing it! I cared more about getting the formula right, than I did about knowing my Father's heart in an intimate and face-to-face relationship. I didn't fully realize why Jesus saved me and what He had brought me into! I had known Jesus as my Savior and my Lord, but I didn't know Jesus as a person. I didn't know God as my Father; I didn't know the Holy Spirit as my constant friend. I could have said all these things were true, but that was purely from a knowledge perspective. I knew it, but I had never experienced it. I accepted it as truth, and I was saved, but I completely missed that truth is not a set of facts, Truth is a Person!

Galatians 3:21-27 in the Message version says this about the law and our own attempts at righteousness:

> If such is the case, is the law then, an anti-promise, a
> negation of God's will for us? Not at all. Its purpose was
> to make obvious to everyone that we are, in ourselves,
> out of right relationship with God, and therefore to show
> us the futility of devising some religious system for getting
> by our own efforts what we can only get by waiting in
> faith for God to complete his promise. For if any kind
> of rule-keeping had power to create life in us, we would
> certainly have gotten it by this time. Until the time when
> we were mature enough to respond freely in faith to the
> living God, we were carefully surrounded and protected
> by the Mosaic law. The law was like those Greek tutors,
> with which you are familiar, who escort children to school
> and protect them from danger or distraction, making
> sure the children will really get to the place they set out
> for. But now you have arrived at your destination: By
> faith in Christ you are in direct relationship with God.
> Your baptism in Christ was not just washing you up for
> a fresh start. It also involved dressing you in an adult faith
> wardrobe - Christ's life, the fulfillment of God's original
> promise.

The fulfillment is Jesus. The finished work of Jesus is our finished work. When we believe that we have not yet attained the fulfillment of His salvation, we will look to what we can control in our own strength to get the myriad of answers we need to solve our problems. But this requires the underlying belief that Jesus didn't do it all. That Jesus is holding back something from us. That it's up to us to get it right. That's why we look to formulas. They are our form of controlling our lives. They sound like good Christian theology but lack the relationship that Jesus has wanted with us all along. The reason He came was to be with us. He is Emmanuel, God with us.

I have found that the smallest detail of a single word can change an entire belief system.

I studied Greek and Latin root words in school and taught them to my daughters when I was homeschooling them throughout elementary school. Taking a root word and adding just a two-letter prefix can make an entirely new thought.

For example, Americans often use the word etcetera, but pronounce or even spell it, excetera. The Latin root for "cetera" means "the other things." And the Latin prefix "et" means "and." The word etcetera is meant be synonymous with the phrase, "and the other things." Which is exactly the idea it is meant to imply when used. So, when it is said or written as "excetera." The speaker would actually be saying, "out of the other things." Which is an entirely different idea than the intent. This commonly made mistake doesn't disrupt our communications because we understand the nuance of the English language and context in which the incorrect form is used and we can easily decipher the intention of the speaker's use of the word.

Sometimes we can misinterpret the intentions of a word. We can treat words with very different intentions and use them interchangeably, when in fact, they have entirely different meanings. I've seen this happen with Scripture. We group these words or phrases together that we commonly see in the Bible, and we assume these words share the same intention and meaning when they actually speak of radical differences.

God showed me how I had done that specifically with the words people and children. I was sitting at church one day, and God spoke to my heart and said, "I never called the Israelites, children of God."

I really didn't know what to make of that at first. Honestly, I felt a little blasphemous. Weren't the Israelites God's children and now us Gentiles get to be like the Israelites and be God's children, too?

I got home from church and got out my Bible and started reading through to see if I had either lost my mind and needed to start repenting.. As I searched for "children of God" "child of God" and any other search words I could think of, I couldn't find anything of reference in the Old Testament to the Israelites that matched that description. I had just always thought that the terms "Israelites" and "children of God" were interchangeable.

I found reference after reference in the Bible of the terms, My people and the children of Israel, referencing the Israelites in the Old Testament. There's a significant difference from those terms to the term, children of God.

There wasn't really a frame of reference for the Israelites to expect anything more than the relationship of a king and his people.  This relationship would be one of distance and impersonal. It was in Scripture and being prophesied of the Messiah and the restoration of God's original intent for mankind, but the Israelites would have needed the Holy Spirit to have the understanding of what this restoration would mean.

The Israelites always wanted a king. When the Israelites escaped from Egypt, they were a group of refugees without a home, or a place to belong. They were wanderers. And even though this was not what they wanted, as we all know, wandering is exactly what they did for 40 years. They wanted land of their own and a king to give them their identity.

Exodus 19 puts us at the point at which Moses and the Israelites had reached Mount Sinai. It had been three months since they had left Egypt. They had seen God rescue them from the Egyptian army. They witnessed a battle fought for them when God parted the sea and they walked through on dry land as Moses held his staff high. They had seen God destroy their enemy, Amalek, as Joshua led the army while Moses, again, raised His hands. They had eaten the manna from heaven and eaten the raven. They had drunk of the bitter water turned sweet by an ever-patient God to quench their thirst and survive. God told Moses in verses 3-6 & 9( MSG):

> Speak to the House of Jacob, tell the People of Israel: 'You
> have seen what I did to Egypt and how I carried you on

> eagles' wings and brought you to me. If you will listen
> obediently to what I say and keep my covenant, out of
> all peoples you'll be my special treasure. The whole Earth
> is mine to choose from, but you're special: a kingdom of
> priests, a holy nation. This is what I want you to tell the
> People of Israel... Get ready. I'm about to come to you in a
> thick cloud so that the people can listen in and trust you
> completely when I speak with you.

The voice of God is in His presence. God was not going to allow all of Israel into His presence, but they could listen from afar. God made very specific guidelines and rules that had to be followed exactly for the Israelites protection. These were the final instructions for this meeting between God and His people in verses 9-13.

> Go to the people. For the next two days get these people
> ready to meet the Holy God. Have them scrub their
> clothes so that on the third day they'll be fully prepared,
> because on the third day God will come down on Mount
> Sinai and make his presence known to all the people.
> Post boundaries for the people all around, telling them,
> "Warning! Don't climb the mountain. Don't even touch its
> edge.

It was on this third day, that God gave the Mosaic law, the Ten Commandments.

The Israelites had to scrub their clothes clean to even be able to just hear from afar the thunder from Mount Sinai as God delivered the Ten Commandments to Moses. But there was no touching the mountain. There was no change of clothes. They were not to enter into His Presence.

No amount of scrubbing could ever wash off from their clothes, or ours, the separation and the sin. No amount of scrubbing could ever make us His children. The same old clothes, though scrubbed, could never turn them from a people to a family. They could hear from afar, but they couldn't get close enough to touch. They could not cross into His presence.

The Israelites were terrified of the Presence of God. The very reality

What was
and is true of Jesus
*could now be*
*true of us.*

they needed to encounter, they were afraid to witness. In their human understanding, they assumed that fear was because of an angry God who expected perfection. But that fear was an expression of what their minds could not comprehend, but their spirits knew all too well. Their fear was the result of the spiritual death of humanity that left a chasm of sin separating God from them.  The Israelites feared for their lives because they knew they could not stand blameless before the Holy One.  They were willing to risk Moses' life, in hopes that Moses could advocate for them. More than just wandering in the desert, they were unable to be in the presence of God. And the reality of this exposed the truth that  not only could they not enter the presence of God because of their own sin, but that even as God's own people, they were still orphans.

Jesus didn't come so we could be like the Israelites. God didn't send His Son to make us His people, He was making us His very own children. Jesus came so the gentiles and Israelites alike could have what He had. He came from the presence of God to bring us back with Him into the Presence of God.

Romans 9:6-8 of the Amplified translation says this:

> However, it is not as though God's Word had failed
> [coming to nothing]. For it is not everybody who is a
> descendant of Jacob (Israel) who belong to [the true] Israel.
> And they are not all the children of Abraham because they
> are by blood his descendants. No, [ the promise was] Your
> descendants will be called and counted through the line
> of Isaac [though Abraham had an older son]. That is to say,
> it is not the children of the body [of Abraham] who are
> made God's children, but it is the offspring to whom the
> promise applies that shall be counted [as Abraham's true]
> descendants.

The NLT says verse 8 this way, "This means that Abraham's physical descendants are not necessarily children of God."

It's the difference between circumcision and crucifixion, partial and whole, associating and belonging. The difference between God's children and God's people. The blood of an animal only coated the Israelites outer works. The blood of Jesus pushed out the blood of fallen man and is now the very blood that runs through our veins. Child of God is not just a pronoun. It's the reality of a birth and lineage that could only be made possible by the Son who belongs in the Presence of God.

The third day of this washing process for the Israelites in the wilderness was the culmination of this holy meeting and resulted in a code of laws required of the people of God. But, there was a better third day when a better covenant was made . And this time, we didn't need to wash our old clothes. Instead, Jesus hung naked on that cross on the top of Golgotha so that we could put on His clothes.

The righteousness that clothes the Risen Savior is the righteousness He has put on us. Though we never earned it, He gave it to us freely. The Presence of God is our home.  We no longer must be kept from touching that mountain. The reality of separation was made untrue by the Truth, Himself. What was and is true of Jesus could now be true of us.

The Presence that we have been saved into speaks to our identity because only those who have been made the righteousness of God can be in the Presence of God.  The intimacy of being in the Presence of God can only be experienced in the relationship of family. When the same blood that flows through His presence flows through our spirits we are rightful heirs to His Presence.

We can look for Him in the physical realm and see Him with our physical eyes, but better communion is being in the Presence of God, spirit to spirit, because you are a child of God. Recognizing that the intimate presence of God is where Jesus has placed you, will empower us to live as Jesus lives. Jesus wants you to know Him in the most intimate way.

This first mention of this new intimacy came when Mary first saw Jesus risen. He gave us this new reality when He spoke these words, "'I am ascending to my Father and your Father, to my God and your God.'" John 20:11-17 (NLT)

Becoming a child of God could only come from the Son of God. He would have to break open of Himself in order for us to be grafted into His Sonship. His Father is now our Father, too. This is who you are, because it is who Jesus has always been. Being in the Presence of God is now your birthright.

The intimacy of being in
the Presence of God can
only be experienced in
*the relationship of family.*

He broke the bread of His body so that we could become His Body. And for Jesus to let us partake in what only He could have before, is a constant reminder of His sacrifice.

The communion elements are symbols of His blood and body, poured out and broken for us. When you take communion, you are actively declaring the identity of Christ becoming your identity. And His Spirit is the seal of that birthright that gives us access to His Presence.

"See what an incredible quality of love the Father has given us, that we should be permitted to be named and called and counted the children of God!... Beloved, we are [even here and] now God's children." 1 John 3:1-2 (AMP)

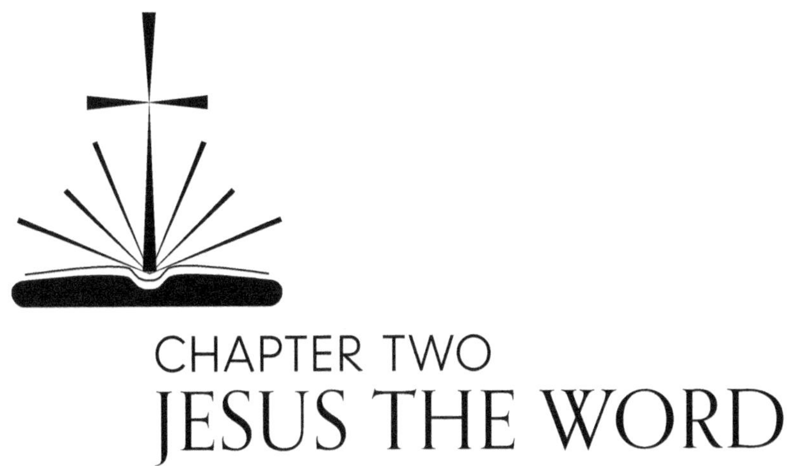

# CHAPTER TWO
# JESUS THE WORD

"Repent, for the Kingdom of Heaven is at hand." Matthew 3:2 (ESV)

For many of us, that sentence can evoke an uncomfortable sense of urgency to get our lives straight. There's a picture in our minds of a punishment coming to us at a speed that is unrelenting. If we don't clean up our acts now, we'll get what we deserve for the sins we've committed. This sentence is seen as a notice of intent to punish us. We look at this proverbial pink slip and think to ourselves, I have to save myself. I have to repent.

The Pharisees looked at the scriptures, Jesus looked through the scriptures. If someone handed you a pair of sunglasses and you only ever looked at them, the sunglasses would be useless at shielding your eyes from the sun. But, if you instead, put the sunglasses on and looked through them, the sunglasses would be used properly in order to shield your eyes from the sun. So it is, with the scriptures. Having the Law of Moses could either be looked at as a way to earn your spot in the kingdom of heaven, a list of rules, or the Law of Moses could be looked through to see your need for a Savior. Looking though the Scriptures would direct your eyes to Jesus. Like tunnel vision, you would see there was only One Way.

In John chapter 5:37-39 (NLT), Jesus states to the Pharisees, "the Father who sent me has testified about me Himself. You have never heard his voice or seen him face to face, and you do not have His message in your hearts, because you do not believe me- the One He sent to you. You search the Scriptures because you think they give you eternal life. But the Scriptures point to me!"

The Pharisees perspective of the scriptures was basically a list of rules. Ultimately, they felt they could control themselves and therefore become their own source  for salvation. According to their theology, their savior would be their good behavior.

Galatians 2:16 says,"we know full well that we don't receive God's perfect righteousness as a reward for keeping the law, but by the faith of Jesus, the Messiah. His faithfulness, not ours, has saved us, and we have received God's perfect righteousness." (TPT)

There is a difference between innocence and righteousness. Innocence is a result of your choices while righteousness is a result of identity.

I was reading through Galatians not too long ago when I came across something I had never realized before.

> My old self has been crucified with Christ. It is no longer
> I who live, but Christ lives in me. So I live in this earthly
> body by trusting in the Son of God, who loved me and
> gave himself for me. I do not treat the grace of God as
> meaningless. For if keeping the law could make us right
> with God, then there was no need for Christ to die.
> Galatians 2:20-21 (NLT)

What I realized reading those verses was that innocence according to the law does not equate to being the righteousness of God. Innocence and righteousness are not the same thing. Even if someone were to have kept every law, their innocence would not be counted as righteousness. Their good behavior would not give them the new identity as a Child of God. Only righteousness could give them this new identity. And as 2 Corinthians 5:21 (NIV) says, "God made him who had no sin to be sin for us, so that in him we might become the righteousness of God."

———

Righteousness
would *require*
a new identity.

———

Righteousness would require a new identity. Innocence would not be made by adherence to the law. True obedience and innocence could only come from righteousness. Jesus lived a sinless life out of His identity as the Righteousness of God.

Jesus knew that it wasn't a matter of people becoming good enough to attain entrance into the kingdom of heaven. The kingdom of heaven had to be brought to them. The kingdom of heaven was at hand. Jesus was there to change everything. There had to be a connection made that was once broken. They needed a cycle of life that started from God, was sustained by God, and went back to God. They didn't need to be better or do better. They needed to be rescued. It was a paradigm shift in the way man thought and perceived. It was not about rules; it was about a family.

Jesus knew what we needed before we did. The religious leaders in the Bible who rejected Jesus as Savior didn't understand that what had been lost was not innocence, it was our connection to Life that had been lost. Which resulted in the loss of innocence. When there is no knowledge of good and evil, there is no sense of innocence because there is no sense of sin. Becoming a child of God breaks the power of sin over us and brings our spirits into unity with Him. I love what Christine Caine said: "Christianity is not about behavior modification, but heart transformation." It's a blood transfusion. His blood adopting us as His own body.

Jesus was more focused on people's hearts than their behavior. He knew that the way we were designed was to function from a connection to Him. And out of that connection, behavior would follow. Our hearts do not follow our behavior. Our behavior follows our hearts.

Jesus had the perspective of FROM heaven to earth. He was in the Father and the Father in Him. That is how Jesus lived. Connected to God. Jesus said He did and said nothing apart from what He heard the Father say. Jesus was saying to the crowds just prior to those verses in John 5, that whatever He sees the Father do, He does. John 5:16-20, "So, Jesus explained Himself at length. 'I'm telling you this straight. The Son can't independently do a thing, only what He sees the Father doing. What the Father does, the Son does. The Father loves the Son and includes Him in everything He is doing." When Jesus talks in John about the life He lives, He's describing the relationship that we

---

Our hearts do not
follow our behavior.
Our behavior
*follows our hearts.*

---

were always meant to have with Him! We were designed to be connected to God. We were designed to live FROM Him as He lives in us! And where the Spirit of the Lord is there is freedom. We were designed to live in freedom. We were meant to live in His Presence.

Repenting was never meant to be our way of controlling our eternal destinies and saving ourselves from imminent punishment. "Repent, for the Kingdom of Heaven is at hand," is Jesus' invitation to us, to be free. To see Him as He is here, at hand. He has accomplished what we never could. This invitation is to turn away from a life that is hindered by good and evil and, instead, into turn to His life, where freedom is boundless and salvation is found in Him. This life He has for us is not measured by what we do, but what He has done. This is, in fact, the way it was always supposed to be.

So, what happened? How did we ever go from how it was meant to be to anything else?

The Biblical account of creation is widely used as a context for the details of how the earth was made, the origins of man, and the evidence of God as Creator. All of this is true, but I believe that there is a greater truth that speaks to our identity. Jesus lived in full awareness of His identity at all times.. He served His Father from a place of Sonship. He didn't work to get to heaven. He was from Heaven. He knew heaven was in Him.

When God created the universe, He gave it its being, its existence, and He gave it its function. He told everything, from the sun and moon to the trees and animals, exactly what their purpose was. He gave each created thing its identity. The entire account of creation in Genesis follows a pattern of first calling each creation into existence, and then speaking into existence the creation's function. God created the world with His Word! When God speaks He creates! When God speaks He breathes life!.

When God created Adam, much more was involved with that creation. God took something He had already made, the dust, and breathed life into it. God breathed His very own life into Adam. Many things were living, but only man was alive. God breathed, and He connected that creation, man, with Himself! Man became alive because he was connected to Life Himself! When He made Adam, the Bible says that God said, "Let Us make man in our own image, according to our likeness." Genesis 1:26. And then, God spoke man's function within the earth. "Let them have dominion over the fish of the sea, over the birds of the air, and over the cattle, over all the earth and over every creeping thing that creeps on the earth." So, God created man in His own image; in the image of God He created him; male and female He created them. Then God blessed them, and God said to them, "Be fruitful and multiply; fill the earth and subdue it; have dominion over the fish of the sea, over the birds of the air, and over every living thing that moves on the earth." Genesis 1:27-28. (NLT)

He spoke out into existence man's function. But, so much more than that, God gave Adam His breath of life. Adam was connected to God in a way that nature and animals could never be. God created man to have a spirit. The Bible says that Jesus is the Life-Giving Spirit. The connection to the Father, even in the garden of Eden, was Jesus! Jesus has always been our One and Only Connector to the Father and the Life that we were always meant to live. The Life that was breathed into Adam is what made his spirit alive. That life can only come from connection to the Spirit of God. This is what made Adam more than a living thing. This is what made Adam spiritually alive.

As we study creation in Genesis, we see that God repeats himself when He's speaking out Adam's identity. But, I believe there's a reason for that. I believe the first time God spoke when He created man's function and purpose, He was bringing that truth into existence. The second time, God spoke man's identity and function, He was saying it to Adam. He was telling Adam his identity.  God had already spoken His plan for man on the earth. He had already spoken man's function and identity and being into existence. The second time He is telling Adam who he is. He was telling Adam his identity. We can only get our true identity from our father!

At the creation of Eve, God made her from something He had already made. He took her from Adam. Genesis 2:21-22( NLT), "So the Lord God caused the man to fall into a deep sleep. While the man slept, the Lord God took out one of the man's ribs and closed up the opening. Then the Lord God made a woman from the and He brought her to the man."

Within that rib, contained the attributes of God that we know to be female. The idea of female did not begin with Eve. What was made in God's image had to already be true about God because as God said, 'Let Us make man in our own image."

And so now, Adam and Eve were there in the garden. Adam and Eve represent God to the earth. They were partners with God. God didn't take charge over nature and living things, He gave dominion over those creations to Adam and Eve. He gave them the place of authority to carry out His will for the earth. His will was for the kingdom of heaven to also be the kingdom from which the earth functioned. And He gave Adam and Eve the connection to His Spirit to not only carry out their identities, but also to choose. By connection of their spirits to His, they had the ability to exercise self-control and live freely in the garden. They lived and breathed the life of God. Their souls were directly influenced by their connection in their spirits to the Spirit of God.

Every fruit-bearing tree was fit for their consumption. There was even a tree of life . That tree provided more than just sustenance. It was their Source. They ate fruit from the tree of life! They didn't have a need for knowing the difference between right and wrong, good and bad, because they lived in God's love. The tree of life was always available to Adam and Eve. They got to eat "life" as much as they wanted! And out of what they received, they lived.

With man and God connected, there was no need to keep spiritual and earthly things apart. The kingdom of Heaven was on earth. And as long as they stayed connected to God, it would remain that way. As long as the Life-Giving Spirit with the breath of God was in Adam and Eve, heaven was on earth. Adam and Eve were the representatives of God the Father, by their connection to the Son of God, Who gives us His Holy Spirit.

As the Bible indicates, life in the garden of Eden went on for a period of time. We don't know exactly how long, but it seems as though Adam and Eve were happy to receive their identities from God and to live with their spirits connected to the Spirit of God. There was unity between man and woman. The unity between them flowed from the unity of the Trinity. When God said in Genesis 1:26, "Let Us make man in Our image. " God is speaking to Jesus and the Holy Spirit. All three were there at creation. God is triune. The Father, the Son and the Holy Spirit. All three are one.

God made man in His image. We have three parts to us. We have our spirit, our soul and our body. You see, there is always unity between God, Jesus, and the Holy Spirit. And God designed for our three parts to not only be in unity with each other, but for our three parts to be in unity with Him. We were meant to live IN Him. Our lives are meant to be sustained by God's Life flowing from our spirit, being connected to His Spirit, to our soul and to our body.  We are designed to live connected to His Spirit and for Him to be our source.

Earth could look like heaven as long as Adam and Eve were connected to God. The Life and kingdom of God was flowing from God to Adam and in turn the earth was in harmony with heaven. God's Spirit was connected to their spirits.  Adam and Eve, though two different people, were made of the same God. And this allowed God's nature to be expressed on earth. You see, God's Spirit, connected to man's spirit, led man's soul and body to be in unity with God's Spirit . He is the Alpha and the Omega, the Beginning and the End. It starts with God and leads us right back to God.  And that is how everything functioned as it was designed to. Adam and Eve believed and behaved according to their God-given identities. And because of that, their souls and bodies were in perfect alliance with God's will.

Adam and Eve had the opportunity to know God intimately. And, as if looking in a mirror, it reminded them who they were every day. They looked like God, in probably more ways than our minds comprehended. And every time they interacted with God, they saw their identity in Him. They knew their Source of Life. They knew Whose they were. He made them. He sustained them.

So, how could Adam and Eve let that change? This brings us back to the trees. You see, the garden of Eden was not a beautiful, utopic  prison. It was a beautiful, utopic home. It was where a family lived. God freely gave them the ability to choose because of His great love for them.

He does not call us His slaves, and not even His people. He calls us His children. He calls us His own. The ability to choose is God-given. God cares so much about your freedom that He designed humankind to have free will. And even though you are capable of using that free will to break the heart of the Father, His relentless love for you will not allow you to be held captive against your will. God doesn't allow your ability to choose to withhold your love from Him to cause Him to withhold His love from you. It doesn't scare Him into trying to control you, because He loves you perfectly.

So, out of all the trees there were in that garden, there was only one that they were told to not eat from. Attached to that tree was fruit that was not intended for food. It was edible and it did look good, but it was not fit for them. The result of eating the fruit that hung from that tree was separation. This tree was the Tree of the Knowledge of Good and Evil.

I've heard this tree referred to many times as the tree of good and evil. But, that's not actually what it was called. It was called the tree of the knowledge of good and evil.  Prior to eating that fruit, Adam and Eve had no knowledge of good and evil. They only knew life. Knowing the Giver of Life.  Being connected to God's Spirit is what kept Adam and Eve spiritually alive. And they knew God as their source. They were not dependent on themselves to sustain themselves. They were sustained by God. Because their hearts, their souls, were being led by their connection in their spirits to the Spirit of God.

The knowledge of good and evil sets us up to make ourselves our own god and our own source.  It gives us our "formula" of how to behave by knowing what is right and wrong. This paradigm allows us to feel in control of our destinies and leads us to believe we have a road map to get from earth to heaven. ,But in reality, any system or achievement that we can maintain in our own humanity apart from God, is inherently flawed.

Adam and Eve could never maintain the earth the way God intended apart from Him. God knew that. He knew that if they ever became separated from Him, they could no longer walk in their true identities and in their true purposes. They couldn't be reminded everyday of who they were. They couldn't see the things that they had always been able to see. Their spiritual eyes would be blinded. And their eyes that could see right and wrong would be opened. There would be death in the place where Life had been. Their spirits would cease to be alive. The partnership between God and man would be broken, and heaven could no longer stay on earth.  There had to be a connection of spirit between God and man. And that's why the serpent wanted Adam and Eve to eat that fruit. He wanted God's children to be separated from God. The enemy wanted man to forfeit his identity.

We know the story; we know Eve ate the fruit and gave it to Adam and he ate it, too. But, I believe there's so much more to this story than our Sunday school classes may have offered.

If we believe that the Bible is meant to be read as a book, then if we have the skill and ability to read, we assume the voice of God is not necessary to read the Word of God. Proverbs 3:5 (MSG) tells us, "Trust God from the bottom of your heart; don't try to figure out everything on your own. Listen for God's voice in everything you do, everywhere you go; he's the one who will keep you on track." "In everything" means everything. Even In reading the Bible, listen for God's voice.

The power that is packed in the Bible is not confined to the words penned by the authors who were inspired by God to write those books. God will take us from glory to glory. He will give us revelation upon revelation. "For the Word that God speaks is alive and full of power [making it active, operative, energizing, and effective]" Hebrews 4:12 (AMPC)

His Word is ever-expanding just as our universe, the world He created with His words, expands. The Word of God is alive and active. If the Word of God is alive, then there has to be breath in it. With the voice of God comes the breath of God. And in the breath of God is life. God breathed on Adam and Eve and made them alive. The Holy Spirit came on the day of Pentecost with the sound of a rushing mighty wind. The Spirit gives life. When Jesus was baptized, the Message version of Luke 3:21 says it this way: "After all the people were baptized, Jesus was baptized. As he was praying, the sky opened up and the Holy Spirit, like a dove descending, came down on him. And along with the Spirit, a voice: "You are my Son, chosen and marked by my love, pride of my life."

Along with the Spirit, came a voice. The Spirit breathes out the voice of God. Without the voice of God, the Bible seems as if a long, flat and oftentimes confusing set of recordings on cultures that seem outdated and barbaric. But, if we read the Word of God with the very Person who is the Word, we are not reading, we are breathing deep. We're stepping into the awareness of the reality of His kingdom and His Presence. The Bible was not designed to be read alone. Because, if we could understand the Bible apart from Him, it would be void of the Life and connection of our spirit to His. It would be void of the power to transform us because we would do it in our own strength instead of His. It would be void of His Presence.

My husband and I have three daughters, Ava, Olivia, and Evre. They are very accustomed to dates with Dad and dates with Mom. Ryan and I take them out on dates all of the time. Those dates can range anywhere from making time at home for playing Monopoly or Uno, to shopping sprees and fancy dinners, and everything in between.  But, what those dates always consist of is face-to-face time between us. It's time for just the two of us. We usually do things all together as a family and that is how we prefer things most of the time, but there's something special about time for them to just be with mom or dad. They value this kind of intimacy so much that they even have nights with just each other. Our girls will pick out a movie together, grab some snacks and they call it a sister movie night. They understand the value of relationship and the inherent intimacy that comes from one-on-one encounters.

When we explain to them what reading the Bible is supposed to be like, we tell them it's like a date between them and God. God will read the Bible with them. It's a special time for just the two of them. It's relational. It's not a Christian chore or box to be checked on their walk with God. It's a time to listen to His voice. To spend time with Him. To have face-to-face communion with Jesus, because He is the Word. When we read the Bible with the Holy Spirit, we breathe in His life and we exhale His life to our surroundings. Jesus said, "The Spirit alone gives eternal life. Human effort accomplishes nothing. And the very words I have spoken to you are spirit and life. "John 6:63 (NLT)  Read the Bible with Jesus, face-to-face. Breathe in and breathe out.

There is so much more to this story in the garden of Eden than merely an account of the fall of man. The fuller story of the garden of Eden will be missed without knowing God's heart and without communion with the Holy Spirit. The fuller story is the loss of man's identity. If we miss that the identity of Jesus is the only identity to pursue, then we can potentially build our Christian lives around a theology that keeps us from walking in all that Jesus came to give us. We can be distracted from living the abundant life that is

The Bible is an
invitation *to revelation
in His Presence.*

ours in Jesus if our understanding of our identity and the identity of Jesus is predicated on a lie that begs our acceptance of separation.

If we're not careful, we will study these scriptures to find finite boundaries by which to live. We will consider the Bible to be a beginning and an end to give us the measurements to map out a successful Christian life. If we're not careful, we will look at the Bible for what we need to become experts at living a well-controlled life. Adam and Eve started to dissect the words spoken, rather than pursue the Presence that spoke them. How often have Christians looked at the Word of God as a code to crack rather than an open dialogue of conversation to have with Jesus? The Bible is a gift is that meant to be relational between you and God. The voice of God will not contradict it. The voice of God holds both Spirit and Truth. The Bible is an invitation to revelation in His Presence.

If we believe the purpose of the Bible is finite, then we would find every answer and the key to our happiness by the merits of our own study. Why then would His presence be important? Why then would His voice be relevant? We could know what was right, what was wrong, and the consequences of both in order to map out our own destiny. We could manipulate and formulate that which we presumed to control. This ideology would position us to function apart from God. We would become our own source. And, in fact, that is exactly what happened.

When sin happened, separation happened. Sin is really death by separation from God. This death decayed into a sin nature. Adam and Eve disconnected from their Source, and instead focused on the tree of the knowledge of good and evil. But, when you think about all they had in the garden, you can't help but ask how it could have come to that? How could they let it go that far? The answer to that question is the same for every sin that has ever been committed. For every bondage, for every addiction, for every fear, for every idol, it all starts with a lie.

# CHAPTER THREE
# JESUS THE TRUTH

The devil had a plan of attack. He didn't just wing it one day. He knew what God had said to Adam and Eve, and he perverted it. God told Adam in Genesis 2 that he could freely eat of every tree in the garden, except one. The tree of the knowledge of good and evil, was that one exception. It was placed in the center of the garden right next to the tree of life. The tree of life was always available to them. God wasn't withholding any good thing from them. But, He loved them and honored them and gave them free will. After all, they had been designed to live in freedom. God gave them all they needed to abstain from the fruit that hung off that one tree. He told Adam that if he ever chose to eat that fruit, he would surely die.

God didn't put Adam at a disadvantage by telling him he would die. He didn't leave Adam confused, thinking He meant a physical death. No human had ever died at that point, so death had a different meaning to Adam, just as life had a different meaning to Adam. Adam ate life from the tree of life. He was spiritually alive. He was breathing the breath of God. Life was communion with God without separation from God.

God did not set them up to fail. Satan would love to make people believe otherwise. The devil is opportunistic. He cannot create. Only God can create. Satan perverts. He distorts. He tries to take what is true and twist it into a lie to convince you of something. Because, before we ever sin, we must first be convinced that the sin is what's best for us . In order for us to disconnect from God's will, we must first be convinced of two lies: a lie about who God is and a lie about who we are.

The serpent asked Eve, Did God really say this to you? Should you really be restricted from this? You deserve this fruit. You don't need to be told what to do. You can do this on your own. You don't need God.

He also told her lies about God. He was trying to convince her that she couldn't trust God. The devil wanted to convince Eve that God had ulterior motives, that He wasn't trying to protect them, that He was trying to keep them from what would truly bring them freedom. The perspective the devil was feeding to her was the false idea that God was imprisoning them. The truth was that God valued their freedom to such a degree that the two trees were side by side and equally accessible. The truth was that freedom was already inherent for Adam and Eve. The devil lied to Eve about who she was, and he lied about Who God is. And verse 6 of chapter 3 in Genesis tells us, "The woman was convinced". (NLT)

Eve saw the tree was beautiful and its fruit looked delicious, and she wanted the wisdom she believed it would give her. There's a reason why Satan chose Eve over Adam. I believe that some of what consisted in the rib of Adam's that God used to make Eve, was the inherent inclination to wisdom. Wisdom is always referred to as female in the scriptures. God has given the female mind a unique ease and fluency when it comes to wisdom. Of course, men can equally share in the wisdom of God, and Solomon had an acute desire for the wisdom of God. But, interestingly enough, Solomon acquired much of his learning from his mother. His mother's wisdom influenced him enough that he wrote her words of wisdom in the 31st chapter of Proverbs.

I believe Satan was going after the God-given desire Eve had for wisdom, and he used it against her. The devil perverted that hunger in her that was for constant connection to the wisdom of God, and instead lied to her that she would only be satiated with the fruit of wisdom from the tree of the knowledge of good and evil. Knowledge can be left to faulty interpretation. Wisdom from God comes with His life and Spirit abounding in it.

———

The reality of earth
around you is inferior
to the *reality*
*of heaven in you.*

———

The idea that eating of this fruit would set her apart to make good choices for herself was the devil's way of twisting the God-given desires for responsibility and self-control. He perverted them into a self-powered fight to hold onto everything in her own hands. He convinced her to be the keeper of her own destiny and to value the answers to life over the presence and the voice of God.

Believing the deception that the wisdom she longed for was wrapped in that forbidden fruit, she took of that fruit and ate it. Then Eve gave some to Adam, who was with her, and he ate it, too. .

Eve was a gift to Adam from God. She represented wholeness and completion to him. And, in my opinion, it seems that Adam must have revered Eve as being very wise and perhaps relied on her for the wisdom that she carried. She was good and perfect in Adam's eyes, because every gift from God is good and perfect. But we all have the ability to turn any gift from God into an idol. I believe that Adam confused the gift with the Gift-Giver. And because of this deception, Adam turned Eve into an idol, and they were both convinced to eat of the forbidden fruit.

The devil convinced Eve that the tree was keeping her from being free, when the tree in fact, was set next to the tree of life to give her the freedom to choose. The two trees side by side represented God's commitment to their freedom.

Eve was convinced that eating this forbidden fruit would make her like God, when the truth was that she already was like God. God had made her in His image. The devil was trying to convince her she needed to attain something she already had. Eve was convinced that she was trapped in a life that was powerless. She was convinced that there was abundant life on the other side of that fruit, rather than the truth that she already had abundant life.

The truth of the life that we have in Jesus, and the truth of our identity has been attacked by the lies of the enemy. The devil has been trying to convince the children of God that they are powerless. He's tried to make them believe that only when they get to heaven will they have abundant life. But, we can't attain heaven on our own, and that's not even the goal for children of God. Heaven was brought to us. And when Jesus made you a child of God and a joint heir with Him, your reality changed. The reality of earth around you is inferior to the reality of heaven in you.

The devil is trying to distract us from who we already are and what we already have so that we never leave the place of trying to attain heaven. Jesus brought heaven and adoption into His family with Him. This adoption, though entirely legal, is not just one of truth, but Spirit and Truth. This adoption is by blood. We don't have to strive to get to heaven. Heaven was brought to us. Jesus came and warred for our freedom. He did what we could not. We have been born to His family to bring heaven to earth. That's where we're seated, and that's where we function from.

If we live our lives on this earth with a perspective of having to attain, to strive to break the barriers to get ourselves to heaven, we will never live in the rest and freedom of our inheritance here and now. We'll assume a job that could never be done on our own. We couldn't even come to Him without Him first coming to us. And, if we continue to believe the lie that tells us we are our own source, we will never carry out our identity and function to this earth. Our identities in Jesus show us our commission to bring heaven and to carry His Presence to a lost world. Our identities beckon us to distribute the heavenly reality that is ours here and now, to the world around us.

We are the ones who have been marked by His name, sealed by His Spirit, covered in His blood. We are the ones whose veins course with the bloodline of our Father. We have His life inside of us. The Life that is the Light of men lives in us! Jesus lives in us! Freely we have received, freely we give.

But, if we continue to believe that we are at a disadvantage on this earth and what we really need still has to be attained, then we will miss why we are here on earth. That would put us on very dangerous ground because, again, it would leave us to trust in ourselves to get from earth to heaven. Knowing the rules, knowing the formulas won't get us there. Good decisions won't get us there. Perfectly executed equations won't produce the answers. And answers won't create salvation. The notion of needing to get to heaven won't get us there because Jesus already came. And He brought heaven with Him. Eve didn't need to become like God; she already was made in His image. If we don't know the identity of Jesus, we will never know ours. We will never see ourselves clearly, unless we see His face.

We will never see
ourselves clearly,
*unless we see His face.*

Someone who is walking through their lives without accepting Jesus and His salvation has believed lies about themselves and about God. They've believed things like, I don't need God. God doesn't exist. There are many ways to heaven. Jesus is not the only way. If I'm a good person , I'll make it. God doesn't want me. I would need to clean up my act before I could ever expect God to want me.

It's staggering to think of how a root lie of being your own source can grow into so many false conclusions.

Someone who has accepted Jesus as their Lord and Savior, but who is constantly battling a particular sin, an addiction, a stronghold, has believed a lie. Maybe the lie is that this is just who they are. Maybe they believe that God has doomed them to this life, and it can only get better once they go to heaven. Or, they think this is just their lot in life. They've believed the victory that Jesus has is locked away in heaven, and they've forgotten that heaven is the very place they're seated in here and now.

Someone who has accepted Jesus as their Lord and Savior, but who constantly looks to formulas, rituals, and is more concerned about rules than a relationship has believed something like, I'll never be enough. They believe that just coming home to their Father isn't enough for God. They believe that God will be angry with them, withhold His goodness from them, unless they get it just right.  They see God as a task master, not a Father. They see themselves as the one who will make everything happen and that God is distant. They've forgotten that we receive the kingdom like children. And a child needs no formula or ritual to be in the presence of their parents.

Someone who, through absolutely no fault of their own, was victimized as a child, maybe even by their very own biological father, may believe that that's all they deserve, and that God is scary and cruel and can't be trusted. They believe that there is no such thing as good and pure love, much less, that God is love.  And they live their lives in torment, loneliness, failed relationships, insecurity, fear, bitterness or anger. They've forgotten that God is not just their God, but that God is their Father. And no amount of human unfaithfulness will nullify His faithfulness.

Sadly, this is not an exhaustive list of the lies that people have believed about themselves and about God. It's just a small portion of the deceit that has led so many people to live as if there is no hope. Each one of those people that I just described are living their lives coming from a perspective of disconnect between heaven and earth. And a vicious cycle is in play. They let something or someone, other than God, tell them their identity. It's a false identity, but to them, it's all they see. They are convinced.

But, Jesus came, and brought heaven with Him! Jesus came and said, you were meant for more! Jesus said, you have a place in the kingdom of heaven. You can eat from the tree of life again. You can eat of me! Jesus is the True Vine. He is the bread that came from heaven. We don't have to strive; we need only rest in Him. To abide in Him.

We were created for more! We can be saved and still miss out on the abundant life that God has for us on earth. Yes, we're saved, and our spirits are saved. We'll spend eternity in heaven. But, we don't have to wait to see heaven. Heaven came to us, and God wants the earth to look like heaven just as He created it to be in the very beginning. He wants us to live in the freedom that He designed us for. We don't have to believe the lies, instead we can know the truth and the truth will set us free! Because, remember, truth is not a set of facts, it's a Person! And Jesus is the life-giving Spirit! He wants us to live in the abundant life He won for us here and now. Heaven is at hand. Jesus lives with heaven in Him. And if Jesus is in us, then heaven is in us as well.

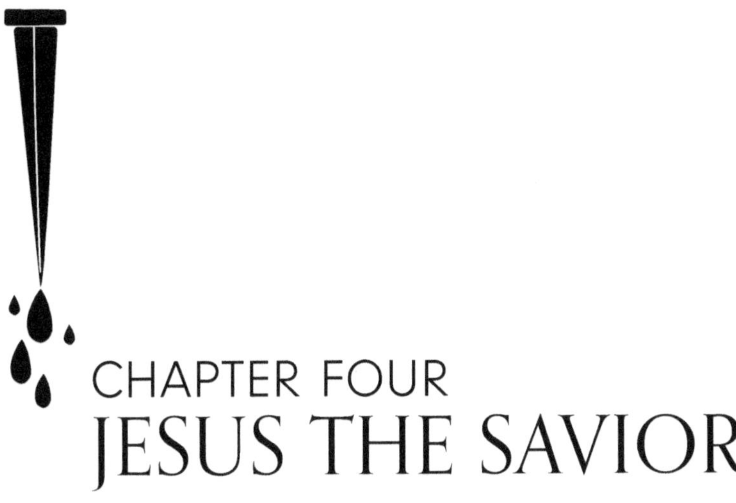

# CHAPTER FOUR
# JESUS THE SAVIOR

This is salvation. The Spirit of adoption, by which we cry out Abba Father gives you your identity. This is who you are. When you received salvation, you didn't just receive a ticket to enter heaven when you die. You received His Spirit. You were born into His presence. The moment of salvation, the actual act of salvation is most accurately shown when Jesus led His disciples into salvation. Jesus gave us a behind the scenes look at what actually happens when we cease to breathe only the oxygen on earth, and breathe in the breath of God to bring us to life. This is your story, too.

It had been 3 days since Jesus was crucified. The disciples had locked themselves in an upper room. Desperate and confused, they were hiding. And through the wall, came Jesus Himself, standing there in front of them.

> But suddenly Jesus appeared among them and said, "Peace to you!" Then he showed them the wounds of his hands and his side -they were overjoyed to see the Lord with their own eyes! Jesus repeated his greeting "Peace to you!" And he told them, "Just as the Father has sent me, I'm now sending you." Then, taking a deep breath, he blew on them and said, "Receive the Holy Spirit..." - John 20:19-22 (TPT)

This was the moment of their salvation. Now, not only did they believe Jesus was the Son of God, they knew He had died and they believed that God had raised Him from the dead. That was the moment they took their first breath. It was the breath of God. His presence, His spirit. This is what took place at the moment of your salvation. You breathed your first breath. You received His Spirit.

This was not the baptism of the Holy Spirit. It would be easy to confuse the two. I think there's a false belief that you can receive salvation but still not have the Holy Spirit. This perception is keeping so many Christians from realizing their true identity. The Holy Spirit is just as much God as the Father and the Son. It is by the Spirit that you are saved. Salvation means more than heaven. It means being of the bloodline of Jesus. It means being His child. Salvation is your spirit coming to life in His. There is no distinction between the two because there are no longer two, but one. The same spirit that raised Christ from the dead lives in you. You don't have two spirits. You gave up the dead spirit to come to life in His Spirit.

Jesus hung on the cross and said to the Father, "Into your hands, I commit my spirit." This is Jesus making your offering of a dead and broken spirit possible by giving the Father His, so that you could do the same. So, just as Jesus has been raised to new life, so have you.

Plainly said, "By living in God, love has been brought to its full expression in us so that we may fearlessly face the day of judgment, because all that Jesus NOW is, so are we in this world." 1 John 4:17 (TPT)

I have a beautiful friend named Lindsay. I was at her house a couple of years ago to get a recording of a testimony in her life that I am so excited to share later in the book, and she said something that was so profound. She started talking about how Jesus appeared to the two men walking on the road to Emmaus after He had been raised from the dead, and how they didn't recognize Jesus. (Luke 24) And she shared a revelation that she had been given. Lindsay said, "Jesus was teaching them a new way of seeing Him."

It was like time stood still. When she said that, I was flooded with revelation. It wasn't just Lindsay telling me this. It was Jesus. My heart felt like it had awoken to level of intimacy with Jesus that I didn't even know existed.

At this time in my life, I was seeing Jesus more intimately than I ever had before. He was deepening my view of Him. He was calling me into a passionate encounter. Not just a one-time experience, but a new way of living. Yes, I had been saved. Yes, I was filled and baptized with the Holy Spirit. Hearing His voice wasn't a new concept; it was a daily encounter. But He had more for me.

He was calling me into a place where I saw His spirit enveloping mine and I became more aware of His Presence in and all around my spirit. No separation between Him and me.  This place is heaven on earth, a new way of seeing Him.

John the Baptist also had a moment of recognizing Jesus in new and profound way. John, while still in his mother's womb recognized Jesus by His Spirit because John was filled with the Holy Spirit even from the womb. John didn't know Him because he saw Him with his eyes. He knew Him because his spirit recognized the Spirit of Jesus.

John the Baptist didn't see Him that way again until the baptism of the Holy Spirit upon Jesus. John remembered what he didn't know he already knew. This wasn't the first time he had recognized Him in his spirit. This was a moment outside of time that awoke a revelation that had first been revealed to his spirit long before. When he saw the Holy Spirit come and remain on Jesus, he instantly knew what he had known from the beginning but could only be perceived in his spirit. He needed to wake in his spirit to recognize Jesus as the Son of God. John was beginning to see Jesus in this new way.

Jesus came to the earth where all things existed because of Him and yet the world did not recognize Him. When Jesus rose, He wasn't recognized at first by the very people He had spent so much time with before. He was speaking to them, but they still didn't recognize His face.

Those two men traveling to Emmaus were walking and   talking about Jesus, to Jesus, and yet they didn't perceive Him. They couldn't perceive that this stranger walking beside them was Jesus because it was now time to recognize Him in their spirits. This wasn't to trick them. This was a call to know Him face to face in the way it was always meant to be. This was an invitation to know Him, Spirit to spirit.

It was time to know His Spirit. It was time to recognize His Holy Spirit. This was the Spirit to spirit intimacy that had yet to be experienced by anyone on this earth other than Jesus with the Father. This is an intimacy that would never be broken. This is a birthright that inherently belonged to sons and daughters of God.

This was how Jesus lived, intimately knowing the Father. Everything Jesus said and did, He first heard from the Father. He lived on this earth in the intimate Presence of God.

John the Baptist knew His Spirit when he was in his mother's womb. When he sensed the Presence of Jesus, he leapt for joy. He didn't have to see a physical face to recognize the One who had called him into being. Our first encounter with the Spirit of God doesn't happen after we are born. He intimately formed you in your mother's womb. He breathed you into being and calls you who you are. When you received salvation, you were not meeting Him for the first time, you were coming back to Him. You were remembering the One who first loved you. You were remembering the One who encountered you in your mother's womb. The words spoken over you when He formed you remain. He is just waiting for you to recognize Him. And when you see Him, you are reminded of the words He had spoken over you when He formed you, when all you knew came from your spirit intimately knowing His Spirit.

The disciples walking to Emmaus had also been walking through three days of confusion, shock, and grief after seeing the death of Jesus. They were trying to make sense of the things they thought they knew. Trying to understand on their own the events that had led to the cross and now hearing of the empty tomb. They were drawn to the words of the Stranger walking with them. As they walked, Jesus carefully revealed the truth of the Messiah written throughout the Scripture. Revealing Truth by Truth. He revealed the truth of the person of Jesus, the sacrifice He made, and the glory He held.

They were compelled to be with this Stranger, still unable to recognize their Savior. The One they had known and seen face-to-face all that time before. They wanted Him to stay with them. They pleaded for Him to stay even though still unaware of the One standing beside them. So, Jesus stayed. He joined them for supper. He took the bread, blessed it, and shared it with

—————

Jesus was thinking of you. He was praying over you. He was speaking out the words that *surround your life and speak into existence your identity*. He has given all that He has and all He is to you.

—————

them. It was in that instant, in that moment, they saw Jesus. They would no longer need to see only a body to recognize Jesus, they would now see with eyes that had been closed for so long, that could see His Spirit. They would know Him face-to-face, Spirit-to-spirit. They were alive again - as alive as Jesus. Their spirits awoke to see Jesus. They awoke to a new life here and now.

The glory of Jesus was revealed. Jesus' prayer spoken out by the Word Himself now permeated throughout the earth, reminding us who He is and who we are here and now. The Spirit-breathed words that remain and hover over the earth are true still, here and now. The glory that was set before Him includes you. Jesus gave of Himself. The true bread was broken, risen, and He has given Himself to you. Jesus is sharing all that He is and all that He has with you. He is the first to share, so we will share. He lives, so we live. His glory, He shares with us so that we can glorify Him on earth. His life, His Word, all that He is, He shares with us. Jesus was thinking of you, and He made a way for you to recognize and remember Him. To see Him face to face. Not just on earth, but heaven on earth. Not just by the sight of our eyes, but by the sight in our spirits alive in Him. The perfect unity in the truest reality. To see who Jesus is, we see who we are here and now. Jesus prayed this for you:

> Father, the time has come. Unveil the glorious splendor
> of Your Son so that I will magnify your glory! You have
> already given me authority over all people so that I may
> give the gift of eternal life to all those that you have given
> me. Eternal life means to know and experience you as the
> only true God, and to know and experience Jesus Christ,
> as the Son whom you have sent. I have glorified you on
> the earth by faithfully doing everything you've told me to
> do. So, my Father, restore me back to the glory that we
> shared together when we were face-to-face before the
> universe was created. Father, I have manifested who you
> really are and I have revealed you to the men and women
> that you gave to me. They were yours, and you gave them
> to me, and they have fastened your Word firmly to their
> hearts. And now at last they know that everything I have
> is a gift from you, and the very words you gave me to

speak I have passed on to them. They have received your words and carry them in their hearts. They are convinced that I have come from your presence, and they have fully believed that you sent me to represent you. So with deep love, I pray for my disciples. I'm not asking on behalf of the unbelieving world, but for those who belong to you, those you have given me. For all who belong to me now belong to you. And all who belong to you now belong to me as well, and my glory is revealed through their surrendered lives. Holy Father, I am about to leave this world to return and be with you, but my disciples will remain here. So I ask that by the power of your name, protect each one that you have given me, and watch over them so that they will be united as one, even as we are one. While I was with these that you have given me, I have kept them safe by your name that you have given me. Not one of them is lost, except the one that was destined to be lost, so that the Scripture would be fulfilled. But now I am returning to you so Father, I pray that they will experience and enter into my joyous delight in you so that it is fulfilled in them and overflows. I have given them your message and that is why the unbelieving world hates them. For their allegiance is no longer to this world because I am not of this world. I am not asking that you remove them from the world, but I ask that you guard their hearts from evil, for they no longer belong to this world any more than I do. Your Word is truth! So make them holy by the truth. I have commissioned them to represent me just as you have commissioned me to represent you. And now I dedicate myself to them as a holy sacrifice so that they will live as fully dedicated to God and be made holy by your truth. And I ask not only for these disciples, but also for all those who will one day believe in me through their message. I pray for them all to be joined together as one even as you and I, Father, are joined together as one. I pray for them to become one with us so that the world will recognize that you sent me. For the very glory you have given to me I

have given to them so that they will be joined together as
one and experience the same unity that we enjoy. You live
fully in me and now I live fully in them so that they will
experience perfect unity, and the world will be convinced
that you have sent me, for they will see that you love each
one of them with the same passionate love that you have
for me. Father, I ask that you allow everyone that you
have given to me to be with me where I am! Then they
will see my full glory - the very splendor that you have
placed upon me because you have loved me even before
the beginning of time. You are my righteous Father, but
the unbelieving world has never known you in the perfect
way that I know you! And all those who believe in me also
know that you have sent me! I have revealed to them who
you are and I will continue to make you even more real to
them, so that they may experience the same endless love
that you have for me, for your love will now live in them,
even as I live in them. John 17 (TPT)

Jesus was thinking of you. He was praying over you. He was speaking out the
words that surround your life and speak into existence your identity. He has
given all that He has and all He is to you. And that includes knowing Him in
a new way that can only come from the intimacy of being one with Him

Knowing Jesus by His Spirit is a deeper intimacy than any physical
recognition. Recognizing Jesus in your spirit speaks to your identity as
the same blood that flows through His presence is the life that flows
through your spirit.  You can look for Him in the physical realm, but better
communion is being in the presence of God because you are a child of God.

Mary Magdalene was the first to recognize Jesus as the Risen Savior in her
spirit. At first sight, she assumed Him to be the gardener. But, as He spoke out
her name, it seems as if Mary's spirit leapt, and she recognized Jesus, Spirit
to spirit. And as soon as she recognized Him, Jesus spoke over her a new
identity as a daughter of God. He said to her in John 20:17 "He's not only my
Father and God, but now he's your Father and God!'"

Jesus gave us what He has: His Sonship. He shares His place in the presence

———

And just like we see our reflection in a mirror, we *see who we are in Him!*

———

of God with us, where our spirits are not just covered by His, but there is no trace of separation anymore, and the truest reality is your complete rebirth as a rightful heir of God.

2 Corinthians 3:18 from the Amplified Bible says it this way, "And all of us with unveiled face, because we continued to behold in the Word of God as in a mirror the glory of the Lord, are constantly being transfigured into His very own image in ever increasing splendor and from one degree of glory to another; for this comes from the Lord Who is the Spirit."

As if looking in a mirror... We look like Him. We look like our Father. When the Spirit of God lives in you, you look like Him. And just like we see our reflection in a mirror, we see who we are in Him! We look to Jesus, and we find our place. We find our identity in Him.

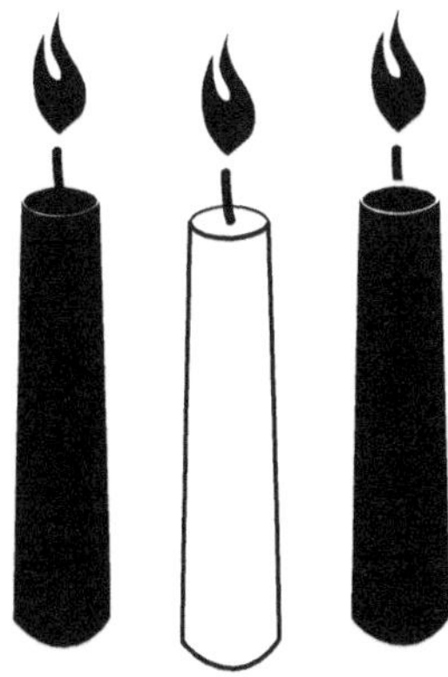

# CHAPTER FIVE
# JESUS THE ONE

At first glance, I probably don't look much like a middle-aged Jewish man.
I'm sure there are few differences between my face and the face of Jesus. Yet,
I look just like Him. I'm actually an exact DNA match. We're not identical
like twins from the same egg but separated. Jesus and His Church share the
same fingerprints. The Church, after all, is His hands and feet. We are the
body of Christ. This is not the idea of just resembling Him. This is being found
in Him. Identical twins can share DNA codes, but through life's experiences,
even how they grow with each movement and touch in the womb, their
appearances begin to change. Subtle differences appear to give even
identical twins their own look. But, we are not twins with Jesus, we exist in
Him.

The redemption and Presence of Jesus shape us into an image that bears His
resemblance even more closely so that when the world looks at us, they
see Jesus. Being redeemed by the blood of Jesus means our spirits are not
just identical to His DNA, but they are also an extension to the lines of code
that cry out His identity . It is His blood that is coursing through our veins.
We are meant to live from the inside out. Our hearts, our souls, are meant to
take every cue, every truth, every perspective from the truth in our spirits.
And within a natural flow, our bodies and actions will continue in this River

of Living Waters, and we'll see Jesus all throughout this earth because we see everything that is true of Jesus, being true of us. This is our true identity.

Identity is such a hot topic right now. It's a sizzle word that tends to attract people. We have seen a drastic surge in recent years of using systems and methods to find our identities. Now, when you tell someone you're an "8 wing 7" no one will wonder what you mean. We have filters on our social media apps that will assign personalities and tell you which Disney princess you are and even identify your celebrity parents. There are so many tools at our disposal. While some of these labels can be found to be helpful, if we're not careful, these labels can give us a false sense of control over our identities. They can even limit us from seeing the unique facet of God that each one of us carries  by stripping our personalities down to a limited number of options.

We were created on purpose and we all want to live our lives with purpose. It's a God-given desire to know our identities. People will bounce from one idea to the next that promises them surety in themselves. They want meaning to their lives that can only be given by their identities. They want to know where they belong and what they can do. We don't want to be orphans. We have a longing for connection. We want a name to attach to ourselves.

When I was young, my favorite movie was Back to the Future. I loved the movie for many reasons, but the biggest reason was my love for Michael J. Fox. Even though I was only 5 years old, I had a huge crush on him. In my bedroom, I had a huge poster with his gorgeous face taking up almost my entire bedroom door. And because of my love for him, I assumed that if Jennifer Parker gets to be Marty McFly's girlfriend, then I most definitely need to look like her.

Jennifer Parker was beautiful, confident, cool, and had the raddest outfit. But, most importantly, if being Jennifer Parker got you Marty McFly as a boyfriend, then that's who I wanted to be! So, when it came time to take my Kindergarten school picture, I knew exactly what it should look like. I made a plan to smile just like Jennifer Parker when that camera clicked. In my 5-year-old mind, I would look most like her if I crinkled my nose when I smiled.  And that's just what I did. I crinkled my nose so hard without even an ounce of embarrassment because I was so sure that I looked just like her in that moment. I'm not so sure that the actress who played that character ever even crinkled her nose in the movie, but regardless, it was her identity I was trying to have.

What's really funny though is that, somewhere along the way, that crinkle stopped being about Jennifer Parker and somewhere over the years, it became a smile that I adopted as my own and make quite a lot! Actually, my husband loves that about me. I guess it really did ultimately get me to my Marty McFly! And even funnier, our youngest daughter, Evre, has perfected the crinkled-nose smile. She has the most adorable way of scrunching that sweet face with the brightest smile you've ever seen and crinkling her little nose.

As cute as it can be for a child to want to emulate someone they find to be fascinating, like me crinkling my nose or little boys wearing their underwear outside of their pants to look like Superman, the search for our identity has been a struggle that the human race has wrestled with since Eden.

As a human race, there have been many sources that we have looked to as authorities on identity. We've looked to our geographical place of origin to tell us who we are. We've looked to our ancestry, creating ethnicities and cultures to define us and give us direction as to what our lives should look like. We've looked to education and employment to define us. We've searched for meaning within our pasts to tell us who we are and what our futures should look like. We've looked to doctors to label us with an identity based on medical conditions. We've allowed our social status to give us our perspective on who we are. We've tried to draw our identity from the possessions we own and the accomplishments we've made. We've allowed our education, or the lack thereof, to  define us. We've allowed governments to tell us our freedoms or our limitations. And we've let ideologies tell us we are oppressors or victims. We've allowed science to tell us we are slaves to genetics.  We look to our gender, our sexuality, or even the color of our skin to find our identity. We've searched anywhere and everywhere for someone to tell us who we are. And we've formed life-perspectives based on those ideas of identity. What we perceive to be reality, we've allowed to be filtered through the lens of the identity we have accepted to be true of ourselves.

Galatians 4:4-6 (TPT) says this:

> But when that era came to an end and the time of
> fulfillment had come, God sent his son, born of a woman,
> born under the written law. Yet all of this was so that he
> would redeem and set free all those held hostage to the
> written law so that we would receive our freedom and a
> full legal adoption as his children. And so that we would
> know for sure that we are his true children, God released
> the Spirit of Sonship into our hearts - moving us to cry out
> intimately, "My Father! You're our true Father."

Our new way of seeing Him. Our new way of knowing Him. Jesus told His
disciples in John 16:23-28 (TPT)

> For here is eternal truth: When that time (once Jesus
> is resurrected) comes you won't need to ask me for
> anything, but instead you will go directly to the Father and
> ask him for anything you desire and he will give it to you,
> because of your relationship with me. Until now, you've
> not been bold enough to ask the Father for a single thing in
> my name, but now you can ask, and keep on asking! And
> you can be sure that you'll receive what you ask for, and
> your joy will have no limits! I have spoken to you using
> figurative language, but the time is coming when I will no
> longer teach you with veiled speech, but I will teach you
> about the Father with your eyes unveiled. And I will not
> need to ask the Father on your behalf, for you'll ask him
> directly because of your new relationship with me. For
> the Father tenderly loves you, because you love me and
> believe that I've come from God. I came to you sent from
> the Father's presence, and I entered into the created world,
> and now I will leave this world and return to the Father's
> side.

Jesus has put us in His position to look and talk directly to God because
we are, in fact, seated with Jesus. Our lives, began with God, are sustained
by God, and our future is with God. His presence is more than a feeling or

spiritual emotion. The word used for presence in the Bible is actually the word for face. It is, in reality, being in the presence of God, here and now.

In 2 Corinthians 3, Paul writes this to the church in Corinth:

Only Christ can get rid of the veil so they can see for themselves that there's nothing there. Whenever, though, they turn to face God as Moses did, God removes the veil and there they are - face-to-face! They suddenly recognize that God is a living, personal presence, not a piece of chiseled stone. And when God is personally present, a living Spirit, that old, constricting legislation is recognized as obsolete. We're free of it! All of us! Nothing between us and God, our faces shining with the brightness of God, our faces shining with the brightness of His face.

When our middle daughter, Olivia, was 2 years old, her primary goal was always to have fun. To her sweet and innocent little heart, every moment should be fun. One of her favorite things to do was to play hide and seek. She was honestly quite good at it. She could find a place to hide and actually stay quiet for as long as it would take us to find her. She would start to giggle just loud enough so we could get ourselves to the corner of the store  she was in, and then she could have even more fun watching us finally figure out where she had been hiding all that time.

But, one morning while we were out shopping, her affinity for fun at all times turned into one of the most terrifying moments of my life. It was a Tuesday, which meant her big sister was at preschool and we were spending some quality time just the two of us. She had a gymnastics class in the morning and then we would typically go somewhere fun afterwards. We were shopping at Target and, as we were wandering through the clothing section, she was happily trailing close behind me. I kept looking back about every 3 seconds, literally. She had finally grown out of the stage where fun to her looked like running in all different directions as fast as she could whenever we were out in public, but I still knew to be on the lookout just in case. I never usually let my kids walk behind me because I always wanted to make sure they were within my vantage point, but it was a slow morning at the store and we were surrounded by racks of clothes, so I felt like we were in a confined enough space with enough barricades to keep us right next to each other, so I allowed it. But I was almost constantly walking with my head turned behind me.

As I looked back to check on her for what seemed like the 90th time, I didn't see her. I quickly started looking 360 degrees thinking that she would have to be right there. I had just seen her about 3 seconds before that and I hadn't seen her run off anywhere. We were at the back of the store with the outer wall right next to us, so I started to spread out and search for her throughout the rest of the section we were in. I was calling her name, and though worried, I thought I would spot her soon. But, then it got a little longer, and a little longer and, still, I couldn't find her. At this point, it had been too long just keep searching on my own. I found the nearest store employee and let her know what was happening. She immediately got on her radio to let the entire staff know to look for her.

All I could think was, whether she would try to walk out of the store of her own will or against it, I would not let her get out of that building. So, as the employee was looking for her, I ran to the front of the store and yelled to the employees stationed there to not let anyone leave the store and to lock the doors. Frantic, I ran back to where I had last seen her and, by now, the other women shopping in that section had taken notice of the situation and they started to look for her, too. As I described to the employee Olivia's tiny 2-year-old frame, her shiny green gymnastics leotard with pink hems and a monkey on the front, her blonde hair and her name, the fear became increasingly intense. She had been right there with me, but now I couldn't reach out to hold her. She wasn't with me anymore. I couldn't see her; I couldn't touch her. We were separated, and that feeling of being separated from my child was overwhelming and all-encompassing. My only goal now was to get to my child. I would do anything to get her back.

When Jesus came from heaven to earth, He came from the presence of God. He had always belonged in the presence of His Father. And when He came to earth, He carried the presence of God inside of Him. He was the point at which heaven and earth met.  He was born of a woman, but conceived by the seed of God. God's very Spirit, saturated in His presence, was the foundation for the earthly life of Jesus where He became fully man and yet fully God. Laying down His deity, Jesus became the first to experience this type of heaven on earth. The seed that carried the separation of sin was not a part of His identity. Even on earth, Jesus lived in the presence of God. He had constant communion with God. The voice of God was His daily bread. The Father's heartbeat on earth was in the heart of Jesus. Death was not a part of His identity, because the reality of death can only be found in the absence of the Presence of God.

Jesus lived every day in the Presence of God. Jesus was born of a woman, but not the seed of Man. He was born of the seed of the Holy Spirit. So, separation from God was not inherent to Him. He lived His life being the First of Many. The many are those who would become children of God. For those who have become children of God, separation would no longer be inherent in them, but rather the presence of God. Jesus did nothing except what He had heard the Father speak. As God spoke, so He would do. He lived in constant communion with the Father. His reality was the reality of heaven. Jesus lived as a boy and grew up in obedience to His parents while in the presence of His Father. Jesus taught in the synagogue in the presence of God. He changed the water to wine, walked on water, fed the hungry, made the mute speak, caused the blind to see, mended broken hearts, healed every disease, defended the ostracized, revealed the purposes of the misunderstood, raised the dead, sweat drops of blood, took the beatings, endured the scourging, suffered the humiliation, and willingly walked the cross to where He would face death... all in the presence of God. In the presence of the Father, He took upon Himself your shame, your guilt, your loss, and your sins. The very last thing Jesus did on the earth was to experience the separation of man and God.

These are the final moments of the life of Jesus before His death as recorded in the book of Matthew 27:46 (TPT)

> For three hours, beginning at noon, darkness came over
> the earth And at three o'clock Jesus shouted with a loud
> voice in Aramaic, "Eli, Eli, lema sabachthani?" - that is, "My
> God, My God, why have you deserted me?"

That was the spiritual separation of Jesus. This was the death that Adam received that cast him out of the presence of God. This was the death that consumed man and was inherent in his seed. The loss of the presence of God was now on Jesus as He hung on the cross. Being separated from Life, the death of the body of Jesus could come.

———

Separation *now had a sacrifice*. Jesus bridged the chasm of sin that separated you from Him.

———

"Jesus passionately cried out, took his last breath, and gave up his spirit."
Matthew 27:50 (TPT)

Never, in all of eternity, had Jesus ever been separated from His Father.
Jesus chose to suffer the death that Adam chose. Jesus took the spiritual
death of separation from the Father. Your separation from God could not
be overcome unless Jesus took it upon Himself. The very thing that caused
Jesus to come to earth was the very thing that caused Him to leave earth:
your separation. That was the reason for all of it. Your separation was your
death. Jesus came to bring you back to life, back to Him, to live always in His
presence. Jesus gave permission for death to come to Him, instead of to you.
Jesus allowed the separation, and the moment God turned away from Him,
was the moment that all things had been placed as a sacrifice to save you.
Nothing compares to the agony of separation from God. Jesus left nothing
undone... to get to you.

"At that moment the veil in the Holy of Holies was torn in two from top
to bottom. The earth shook violently, rocks were split apart, graves were
opened." Matthew 27:51 (TPT)

Separation now had a sacrifice. Jesus bridged the chasm of sin that separated
you from Him. Since the fall of man, the seed of God  was missing from
the earth... until Jesus was conceived of His seed.  And as a seed, He was
given for you. To be the Seed sown to make a harvest just like Him. Sown
to make a family of children born of the same seed. The life of Jesus, living
in the presence of God on earth could now be your life. You could be born
again but not out of seed that caused inherent separation. Instead, this Seed
you are conceived of now as a child of God, born again, brings you into the
presence of God inherently. It's your identity.

His passionate, intense, boundless pursuit to get you back was completed
when Jesus died for you. After all that time of separation from you, God
ripped through the veil that once separated you from Him because nothing
would stop Him from getting to you.

We can sometimes feel like God is a million miles away. We can feel like
we haven't heard His voice in so long and we wonder if He has left us. To
believe that God has turned His back to you, to believe the lie that says
you have to get back into His presence, is to miss the truth of the agony of

separation that Jesus took for you. To believe that you have somehow lost His presence is to forget that Jesus died outside of the presence of God for your birthright to live here and now in the presence of the Father. The Father endured separation from His One and Only Son, so you could also be His son, His daughter. Jesus suffered your very separation, went to hell, but He came back. He ascended and He's with the Father now and always. Not just in body, but in Spirit, He is always with Him. This is what Jesus died for you to have. He died so you could have what He has. He came so you could live as He lived. That as He is, so are you.

You are exactly who Jesus died for. You are specifically why God sent Jesus to earth. God saw your face on the other side of that veil and tore through it to have you in His arms. The presence of God is where you belong. What Jesus endured for you is the reason why you live in the intimate presence of the Father, even when your feelings would say otherwise. The separation Jesus experienced is the very reason why you, at all times, have access to the very same communion with God that Jesus experienced on earth. Living in the presence of God is inherently true about you. Where Jesus is now, you are too. You are the point at which heaven and earth meet.

I'm not sure how long it was that Olivia was missing-probably just a few minutes-but I remember it was unbearable. I couldn't let the separation continue any longer. I couldn't just leave and try to replace her with someone else. She was the only one I needed to rescue. The one I was separated from could not be replaced. She carries the unique spirit that only she can have. There is only one Olivia, and I had to get her back. I would have ripped through anything to get to her.

When we finally heard her little giggle coming from behind a small corner of space between the back of a mirror and the outer wall, I didn't walk, I ran to her. I grabbed her and held with a fervor like never before. As I held her in my arms, I began to cry. The women who had stopped what they were doing to help find her started crying. Those few moments are in no way an accurate depiction of our separation, but just imagine how much God wanted you back. Yes, He came for all of us, but He specifically was coming to save you. There is no replacement for you. You cannot be replaced no matter how many children He has. You are loved as if you are His Only because His Only Son took your place, your separation. Our most fundamental need is to be with Jesus. Our deepest desire is to be with Him. And we would be lost without Him.

This is what Jesus did. This is what it means to be in the presence of God. The presence of God is not just a feeling, it's the reality of who you are and all that you have because of the One who gave all He had and all that He was for you. As He is, so are you.

> Those who give thanks that Jesus is the Son of God live
> in God, and God lives in them. We have come into an
> intimate experience with God's love, and we trust in the
> love he has for us. By living in God, love has been brought
> to its full expression in us... because all that Jesus is, so are
> we in this world.
> 1 John 4:15-17 (TPT)

There was a veil that kept us from seeing Him face-to-face. We couldn't have what Jesus had until Jesus gave up what He had, taking our separation so we could have His connection. He took our death and gave us His life. He went to hell; He took back the keys and made us rightful heirs to the kingdom in Him when He rose and gained the life that is now ours in Him. That veil, that curtain, was ripped. Hebrews 10:21 tells us plainly, "The 'curtain' into God's presence is His (Jesus) body." (MSG)

There was no other way, but the Way. He experienced the separation that was your inheritance as a soul of the fallen world, born from the seed of man. Jesus was born of a woman, but the seed was of the Holy Spirit. Death, sin, and separation were not legally his because He was of the seed of God. He took your separation. He carried everything that is inherent in sin and true of separation from God. But, now He has brought  you into His inheritance as a child of God. Because the presence of God is the rightful inheritance of Jesus, you now have the freedom to rightfully inherit your place in the intimate presence of the Father. This is your inheritance, here and now: His presence, His life. Being born again into the Spirit of Sonship means you are not only an heir but also inherently in the presence of God, because the seed of man does not have legal authority over you anymore. You have been born as a Child of God.

Jesus told His disciples that it was better if He went away because, instead of living with the physical body of Jesus, they were now going to live IN Jesus. They would live in the Spirit by which they would cry out, Abba Father. Jesus is the Life-Giving Spirit.

"For it is written: The first man, Adam, became a living soul. The last Adam became the life-giving Spirit." 1 Corinthians 15:45 (TPT)

When Jesus took that deep breath and breathed into His disciples, they came alive. They came alive to their new identities, their new life in Him. The life Jesus has, He gave them.

This was the moment when the breath of Jesus and the life of Jesus became their breath and their life. This is when those disciples became children of God. As Jesus abided in the Father, unified with the Holy Spirit, now we are unified in Jesus, abiding in Him. His Holy Spirit has made our spirits alive. The breath we breathe is His. The life we have is His. Here and now.

We find our identity in Jesus. We see our place in Jesus. We realize that, though there are many that are in this family of God, each of us is loved as if the only because Jesus came to us as God's One and Only Son.  His Life is your life. This is what you were given and what truly happened when you gave your life to Jesus.

You would be missed if you weren't in the presence of the Father. You are irreplaceable. I could have no more walked away from Target that day thinking I could have just replaced Olivia, than God could have ever stopped pursuing you just to replace you. There is no replacement for you in the Father's eyes or His arms. You are wanted. You were fought for. Jesus died for you to be in the arms of the Father. Just as He is, so are you.

"For it was always in his perfect plan to adopt us as his delightful children, through our union with Jesus, the Anointed One, so that his tremendous love that cascades over us would glorify his grace - for the same love he has for his Beloved One, Jesus, he has for us. Ephesians 1:5 & 6 (TPT)

———

You are the point
at which *heaven
and earth meet.*

———

# CHAPTER SIX
# JESUS, EMMANUEL

That first plan contained directions for worship, and a
specially designed place of worship. A large outer tent
was set up. The lampstand, the table, and "the bread of
presence" were placed in it. This was called "the Holy
Place." Then a curtain was stretched, and behind it a smaller,
inside tent set up. This is called "the Holy of Holies." In it
were placed the gold incense altar and the gold-covered
ark of the covenant containing the gold urn of manna,
Aaron's rod that budded, the covenant tablets, and the
angel-wing-shadowed mercy seat.
Hebrews 9:1-5 MSG

This is the account in Hebrews of the inner part of the tabernacle that was
built under the direction of God through Moses. In the previous chapter,
we talked about the curtain, and how Jesus' death made the removal of that
veil a reality, sharing with us the access that we now have with the Father.
This access is the very access that Jesus has because Jesus didn't step into
the representation of the tabernacle on earth, Jesus went into the very place
itself.

A few verses later in Hebrews, the Bible tells us this: "For Christ did not enter the earthly version of the Holy Place; he entered the Place Itself, and offered himself to God as the sacrifice for our sins... He sacrificed himself once and for all, summing up all the other sacrifices in this sacrifice of himself, the final solution of sin... And so, when he next appears, the outcome for those eager to greet him is, precisely, salvation."

Because Jesus rose, He now breathes His Life into us, which is salvation. Just as the disciples experienced, we too have His Life breathed in us. In this chapter, we're going to focus on another element of the inner part of the tabernacle. We're going to look at the "bread of presence."

It was a moment I will never forget. Words I will always remember. An anointing that I will always carry.

It was mid-morning, and I was in my bedroom, having time just with Jesus. My kids were in the rest of the house playing, and my husband was out of town. It was just me and Jesus. It seemed like a typical morning of reading the Bible with the warmth of the morning light and my door shut, making a dulled sound of the girls playing in the family room. I had been standing in worship and prayer when suddenly the atmosphere in the room changed, and I could feel His presence so strongly. It felt like the King had just entered my bedroom. I immediately dropped to the floor in worship. I knew He had entered the room and all I could think to do was to drop to my knees and bow before Him.

It was a moment. Not just a moment that could be timed on a clock. It was a moment that was working on the time frame of heaven . I knew this moment was one when Jesus Himself was standing right in front of me. He had clearly planned this. I had never experienced anything like this before. I wasn't trying to work up my feelings or create a powerful moment. I wasn't feeling desperate for an encounter or asking for His manifest Presence. Everything seemed normal, until everything changed. Then I heard God say,

*Ask me what I want to say to you.*

This was not a method of prayer I often used. It surprised me that He would ask me to ask Him. I usually didn't need any prompting when I had a question of my own. This was unfamiliar territory. While I didn't have framework for it, I knew that if God had decided to show up of His own accord, I would not waste this moment. I knew that whatever He told me would be words that were going to start something on earth that had started long before in heaven. His command felt sacrificial but I also knew that whatever sacrifice it would be would be worthy of my "yes."

So I asked Him, "What do you want to tell me?"

As soon as I asked, He answered,

*Share the bread.*

I instantly knew what that meant. He wanted me to share what He had been giving to me: The bread of His presence. The revelation words that He had been sustaining me with, He wanted me to share.

There was an inner dialogue that I had been having with Him. In this dialogue, He had drawn me into such a deep and intimate relationship with Him. This dialogue was always telling me of the identity of Jesus. This intimate, continual dialogue that had always been between us, He was now asking me to share.

At this time in my life, God had been revealing so much to me over the few years prior to this encounter. I was receiving revelations that would surprise me, because they were something so new and yet familiar all at the same time. It was a relatively new experience in my life. Not that hearing God's voice was necessarily new to me, but what He was entrusting me with in these revelations was new. I could hardly pick up my Bible without Jesus illuminating something to me that I had never seen before. And often, He would speak something to me, and I would go to the Bible and see that it was in there all along. I had read those verses so many times, but I was seeing Truth in a new way.

In an instant, He would speak something to my heart, and I knew something without having learned it. I didn't realize it when He first started revealing these simple yet profound words, but He was prophesying over me what I was to prophesy to the earth.

The words that He had been speaking to me were my bread, and He wanted me to "share the bread."

When He spoke those exact words, "Share the bread," I knew that the Bible often referred to His words as bread.

But it's not just words that belong to a language formed on earth. It's words that are Spirit-breathed and therefore alive. His words existed in heaven before earth. The words He speaks to us are Life-Giving, and in His Presence is Life. Seeking the Presence of God takes priority, even over seeking His words. Because close to Him, you can hear even a whisper. In His Presence, you will always hear His words. As C.S. Lewis wrote, "But look for Christ and you will find Him, and with Him everything else..." (Mere Christianity)

That day when God told me to share the bread, it spoke so much more than just three words to me. God was giving me something that was alive. It was a seed. But this seed was wrapped in something that was ready to eat now and simultaneously be planted in me to grow and produce a harvest to share.   In that moment, I said, "Yes!" This book is an offering to the Lord. This book is part of that "yes." Jesus commissioned me that morning to share the revelations, the words, and even my relationship with Him with the world around me.

John 6:47 - 48 (TPT) pens these words of Jesus:

> I speak to you living truth: Unite your heart to me and
> believe - and you will experience eternal life! I am the
> true Bread of Life." And in verse 58 Jesus says, "I am not
> like the bread your ancestors ate and later died. I am the
> living Bread that comes from heaven. Eat this Bread and
> you will live forever."  I knew that the bread of communion
> represents the body of Christ, and I also knew that Jesus is
> the Word made flesh.

When the devil tempted Jesus to turn stones into bread, Jesus said, "It has been written, Man shall not live and be upheld and sustained by bread alone, but by every word that comes forth from the mouth of God." Matthew 4:4 (AMP)

That verse is so powerful to me. Jesus is quoting Deuteronomy 8:3 in that verse. He's speaking a truth that so many of us can pass right over without seeing how much depth that verse holds. There are words that God speaks to us sustain us in our daily lives. Are we listening?

Whether it's a scripture that the Holy Spirit breathes in you or a word from God that brings life to your heart for the situation at hand, there's a sustenance provided by the word of God that we are to live by. The way the Bible describes it, God's words are like bread. In taking a deeper look at the significance of bread in the Bible, we get a broader picture of its relevance and a greater understanding of the Word.

Behind the curtain in the tabernacle was where the Holy of Holies was placed. It was the point at which heaven met earth. God would allow His Presence to come and hover in the Holy of Holies. His voice was in His Presence. No one, not even the high priest had an all-access pass to this sacred place. There was a rigorous list of rules and procedures for those who were to enter this place at designated times. The priests would eat the bread that had been in the Presence of God in the Holy of Holies. The bread that had been in the Presence of God was given to them.  God instructed Moses in the book of Exodus to always keep fresh Bread of the Presence on the Table before Him.

There was a time in my life recently that put me through an intense revelation of His Presence. We had made a lot of transitions in a short amount of time and had a few bumps  within the processes. I found myself without my usual safety net of community and I had to put down the ministry work that I had been so involved with in order to make these transitions in our lives as a family.

It was 2017, and our youngest daughter was only a few months old when we made the move from Oklahoma City, Ok to Redding, CA. We had been so excited to begin this next chapter in our lives. God had told us to come to Bethel Church about a year before we moved, and that Ryan would be on staff there but not to pursue it. He just wanted our "yes," and He would take care of everything else. So, that's what we did. We said yes to moving without knowing anyone in Redding or having any connections to Bethel.

The plan was for Ryan to keep his current job and work remotely from Redding and just keep taking the steps God told us to take. We made plans to move by September of 2017 and, though it seemed like a huge risk to all of our friends and family, it didn't feel that way to us. We felt His Presence all along the way and knowing He is faithful and that He was with us made it feel like it wasn't that risky at all. I even remember talking to God before we had moved and telling Him how almost everyone we knew was telling us this was a terrible idea and He responded to me with this: "My word is enough." And it was. Before we even got to Redding, Ryan was offered the position as CEO of Bethel School of Technology. The very weekend that we had planned to move to Redding, Bethel announced the school and named Ryan as the CEO, a school and a position we didn't even know was in the works when we first said yes to being in Redding. It was nothing short of a miracle how God went ahead of us and ordered our steps.

By this point in my life, I had been experiencing an overflow of revelation for a few years and new words that God would give me that were fueling me at an accelerated pace. Yet, in all of the excitement of each word from God, what marked all of them was His Presence. Living in the awareness of God's Presence and sensing His nearness became a constant in my life. But, in the midst of the transition, after a few months in Redding and seemingly without warning, something changed. I knew the Presence of God would never leave me, and I knew was, in fact, was what made me truly alive, but I couldn't sense His Presence anymore. God would still give me prophetic words and insight, but I couldn't sense Him. And I didn't just mean sensing Him in a physical or emotional sense, but in my spirit, I couldn't feel Him. This was truly the darkest I had ever felt. Not sensing His Presence felt like torture. I knew He was with me, but I also knew He was keeping me from experiencing the awareness of His Presence on purpose. This messed with me on so many levels, including my theology. It was like this for about a year. I would spend nights in bed, weeping in pain over not sensing Him. I would tell Ryan how I felt like a messenger, not a daughter. God was still giving me words, but I felt as if I had never been further away from Him.

This season didn't last forever, but it did mark me forever. I later asked God, why He led me through that time without letting me sense His Presence, yet still hearing His voice. And He told me there were two reasons. The first was that He wanted to communicate to me something that I hadn't previously known about myself. He knew that I wasn't after a relationship with Him only for the words and revelation that He would give me, but deep in my heart, I had never had that moment of clarity. That intense time of revelation that I had been experiencing, was a gift, but never meant to replace the Giver.

———

I needed to know that
if God never gave me
another revelation or
word again, that
His Presence
*was enough for me.*

———

You can be fully grateful for the revelation He gives you without letting it become your only reason for communion with Him. I needed to know that if God never gave me another revelation or word again, that His Presence was enough for me. He was bringing me back to first love, and the reason why I valued His words so much, and it was because His words always came within His Presence.

The second reason He gave me was this revelation that He wanted me to discover: follow My Presence, and listen to My voice.

My sheep listen to my voice; I know them, and they follow me." John 10:27 (NLT)

In all of the words and direction that God had given me throughout the years, I had become accustomed to following His voice. And this is good and necessary throughout all of our journeys, but obeying His voice doesn't replace our deepest desire to be in His Presence. If you had asked me prior to this experience, I would have said that following His voice is the same as following Him, but there is a distinction. That verse above notes a specificity to listening to His voice and following Him. Being only obedient isn't the abundant life that Jesus came to give us. Your place in heaven is not of a military command, but a family. You are His child. It could have become very easy for me to only follow His voice. I could have easily decided to come to Him for what He was going to give me and to miss the greatest part of my inheritance, which is Him . Just being with Him. And I needed to share not only the words that He gives me, but the words that He has given me reside in His Presence. And when I am speaking what He is speaking, I'm also communicating the Life that is in His Presence.

God was not far off, and I didn't have to communicate with him as if this was a long-distance relationship just waiting for my next correspondence from Him. In His love for me, He let me see what it was like to only have His voice. He taught me something that was not only true about me, but true of all of us: Nothing can satisfy us like His Presence.

> He took some bread and gave thanks to God for it. Then
> he broke it in pieces and gave it to the disciples, saying,
> "This is my body, which is given for you, Do this in
> remembrance of me. Luke 22:19 (NLT)

To have such deep communion with our Savior as to take of His body sacrificed for us and put it into ours to receive His life, is a closeness that goes far beyond just being near to someone. This is Spirit to spirit. This is His Presence.

The closest thing I can liken this type of Presence-intimacy to would be the physical relationship between a husband and wife. The covenant act of sexual intercourse is a moment of intimacy in which we experience our spouse's presence in a way that requires no words and yet communicates the deepest vulnerability and passion. Even though the covenant of marriage still exists outside of those moments, it's in those moments of intimacy that life is created.

This, of course, does not negate the irreplaceable need for communication through words, and we will be moving into that topic next. There would be no way to sustain a marriage with only sex, even really great sex. But, this does provide a glimpse into the innermost temple, where His Spirit joins with ours. Where His Presence is valued above all else. There is an intimacy in this relationship with God that Jesus shares with you and is fully realized by being in the Presence of God. And in His Presence, there you find everything else.

"Look! The virgin will conceive a child! She will give birth to a son, and they will call him Immanuel, which means 'God is with us.'" Matthew 1:23 (NLT)

Jesus, the Bread of His Presence. Being in the Presence of the Father is because of Jesus. He has put His name on you. He is Emmanuel.

———

Being in the Presence of
the Father is because of
Jesus. He has put
*His name on you*. He is
Emmanuel.

———

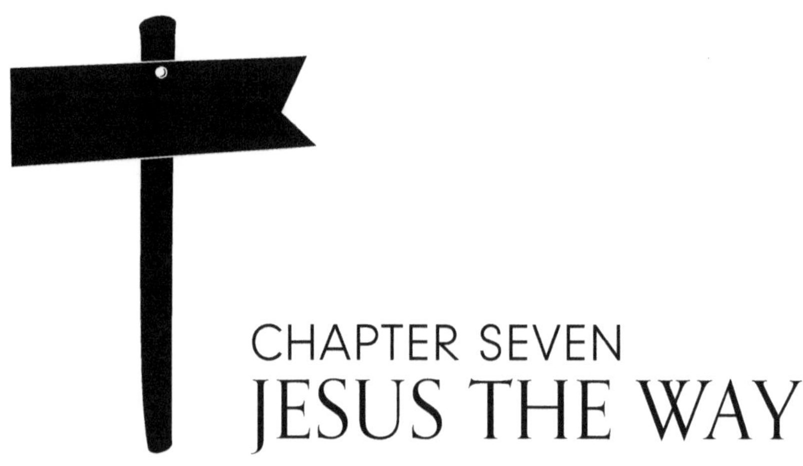

# CHAPTER SEVEN
# JESUS THE WAY

Jesus. He is the Word. He is present with God. He is the Word by Whom God spoke, bringing all creation into existence and calling out creation's identity. He is the Life by which we live. The Light that no darkness can extinguish. The Light that came into this world and lived in the power of God. Not in His own deity, but in the power of His Father Who sent Him. The Son who took on our separation when He fulfilled His call to die on the cross. But, now seated at the right hand of God, he will forever be in His Presence. And the life we partake of, this Bread, is the life that gives us eternal life, seated with Him, in the Presence of our Father.

When Ryan and I explain to our daughters about hearing the voice of God, the Word He is speaking to them, we explain that it's similar to the way he and I speak to them. When we hold our daughters close, when they are in the intimate presence of their parents, we need only whisper for them to hear our voice. They know we are speaking to them. There is more than just an exchange of words. The closeness that brings peace and comfort and the joy of being cherished is found in the arms of the ones who call them their own.

This is how Jesus lived on earth, and this is what we have in Him. This is the abundant life Jesus won for you. "Therefore, brethren, since we have full freedom and confidence to enter into the Holy of Holies in the blood of Jesus, By this fresh and living way which He (Jesus) initiated and dedicated and opened for us though the separating curtain (veil of the Holy of Holies), that is through His flesh..." Hebrews 10:19-20 (AMP).

You can, now, with absolute certainty in who Jesus is, be in the Presence of the Father. And in His Presence, He holds us so close that He needs only to whisper to speak to the ones He holds in His Presence. You are His child. You have been given that identity. And as a child, you are not left without your daily bread. He speaks to you, and you hear Him. It's actually the most familiar voice to you. It's the first voice you ever heard. You are made of His voice. His voice is the voice that called you into existence.

The intimacy that Jesus has with the Father, He has shared with us. Jesus was the first to share His relationship with the Father with us, and Jesus told us in John that, because of our salvation, we will be able to commune with God directly. The Bible describes intimacy as a child of God as "Spirit on spirit, His life on our lives!" (2 Corinthians 3:6). The abundant life that Jesus promises us in John 10 is the abundant life that He himself lives. Because it is His breath of life that we breathe, alive in Him.

Because Jesus defeated separation, His Presence is not only with us, it's in us. 1 Corinthians 6:17 says, "But the person who is united to the Lord becomes one spirit with Him." You belong to God-spirit, soul, and body. Your body houses your spirit. It is the vehicle by which we have a position on this earth. But, our bodies-just like our spirits- are not our own, they are God's (paraphrase 1 Corinthians 6). If your spirit is united with His, then you carry His Presence.

Jesus is the True Bread that came from heaven. He came from the Father's presence. When Jesus laid down his deity, He chose to live in His Presence on the same earth that we are on, and the relationship that He had with Him, is the relationship you and I have been saved into.

John 1 also tells us that Jesus, being the Word, became flesh and He "tabernacled" among us. Jesus became the Living temple of the Holy Spirit. The earthly tabernacle, where the veil separated the Holy of Holies from the rest of the world, and at the tent of meeting is where God's Presence would come and hover. This is where the priests would hear the voice of God. In the book of Exodus, God gave Moses the instructions of a daily communion with Him and details of the sacrifice at the Tent of Meeting. Verses 42-46 tell us, "This is to be your regular, daily Whole-Burnt-Offering before God, generation after generation, sacrificed at the entrance of the Tent of Meeting. That's where I'll meet you; that's where I'll speak with you; that's where I'll meet with the Israelites, at the place made holy by my Glory. I'll make the Tent of Meeting and Altar Holy. I'll make Aaron and his sons holy in order to serve me as priests. I'll move in and live with the Israelites. I'll be their God."

Jesus is the point at which God and man meet. The place of reconciliation. Our Redeemer. The point at which heaven and earth meet. The true tabernacle that makes His Presence our reality and our home. He is how Heaven came to earth.

We see in the old covenant written in Exodus, that God moved into an earthly tabernacle. And that He would speak with them there. That He would meet with them at that tabernacle. This was the point at which heaven and earth met. But, Jesus came from heaven, and made a new tabernacle. He was the point at which heaven and earth met. He had the Holy Spirit inside of Him. Now, we have the Holy Spirit in us. Jesus breathed His Spirit into us. And we can hear the voice of God. He speaks to us, just as He spoke to Jesus.

Jesus, Who is the Word, was with God and He remains with God. And Jesus, the Word, promised you that He would be with you always.

If we remember who we are, we will not forget that our spirit is alive in His Spirit. That there is no more separation between us and Him. And, if no separation, then nothing to keep us from hearing His voice.

You were created and redeemed to commune with God. You can hear the voice of God. He speaks to you directly and you have been given the position of His child to speak with Him directly. This is love. This is who you are.

Seeing our identity in the face of the One who gave it all for us, we see that our example is Jesus. Our example as to the life we can live here and now, is how Jesus lived on this earth. This is how Jesus lived on this earth and has redeemed you to do the same.

We see that Jesus lived His entire earthly life, until He was separated at the cross, with His Spirit connected to the Father's, and in constant communication with the Father. And Jesus prayed that as the Father is in Him and He in the Father, that we also may be one in Them! God loves you as He loves Jesus. Jesus prayed that the love that God had bestowed upon Him, that we would feel that love in our hearts and that He Himself would be in us. What Jesus had access to on earth, you have been given access to. Don't miss this truth.

When Olivia was about four years old, she asked us a question at bedtime one night that turned into a powerful moment between her and God, and for our whole family. We were tucking them in and the lights had already been turned out, and Olivia had a question. She had just watched a movie with "bad guys" in it. We had watched 101 Dalmatians that night. And there were two buffoonish-type bad guys and of course the one really bad guy, Cruella DeVille. These characters brought about a question Olivia had never thought of before. And she asked me, "Are bad guys real?"

This is not, necessarily, an easy question to answer. Yes, I knew what the answer to that question was, but the way that I would explain it to her would be paramount. This moment held the potential to either create a paradigm of fear for Olivia or create a paradigm for her that magnified the reality of heaven over the reality of earth. So, in that moment, I looked at her, took a second to surrender my heart to God to speak whatever it was I would hear Him speak, and I answered her question. I had been praying Psalm 91 over our family for a couple of years. It was a chapter in the Bible that God led me to and told me to pray over our family daily. A couple of months before Olivia had posed this question, God put it on my heart to pray that both Ava and Olivia would receive a personal revelation of Psalm 91.

I'm not a fan of lying to our kids, but I am a proponent of speaking the truth in a way that is appropriate for their age. So, I told her that bad guys are real, but we don't need to be afraid because God protects us. You would think that I would recognize this question from Olivia as the perfect opportunity to talk to her about Psalm 91 and to activate the answer to a request that I had asked of God. But, it just didn't occur to me. I didn't think to connect Olivia's question to me asking God to reveal Psalm 91 to my kids. But, I think I know why I didn't see that opportunity. It wasn't what God wanted me to do. He didn't want me to tell her. He wanted to be the One to reveal His promises of protection to her.

At first, my answer was not what she wanted to hear, and immediately, her thoughts went to - how can I be safe then?.

Psalm 91 is filled with promises of God's protection. And, throughout the years, God has revealed to me deeper insight and given me fresh manna on different sections in this chapter of Psalms. The first verses speak of the Presence of God:

> He who dwells in the secret place of the Most High shall remain stable and fixed under the shadow of the Almighty [Whose power no foe can withstand]. I will say of the Lord, He is my Refuge and my Fortress, my God; on Him I lean and rely, and in Him I [confidently] trust! Psalm 91:1-2 (AMP)

The entire chapter is more than worth a read and applies to this story, but we'll stick to just these verses for a moment. These verses are describing to us how God is our Hiding Place. That we can abide in safety in Him.

I wanted my daughters to know, by the voice of God, and revealed by the Holy Spirit, that He is their dwelling place. That He is with them and that they are found in Him. I asked God that He would give them a revelation of Psalm 91.

As we sat there on her bed and talked about God's protection, Olivia had a moment with God that forever changed her perspective. He gave Olivia a vision and she immediately shared it with us. She said, "Mom, I saw God's arms all around our house!. It's like there's purple all around our house!" And then she said with such confidence and excitement, "GOD IS OUR HOUSE!"

It was such a sweet moment. This is what God spoke to her to bring about truth and love in the face of fear. He is her house! She dwells safely in Him. His arms are around her, and even though we can go to sleep knowing we are safe within our home, our true safety, our true protection, our true home is our Father. He is our house!

God revealed Psalm 91 to Olivia in a way that spoke directly to her, and it ministered to our entire family, too. Olivia didn't know that Psalm 91:4 actually says, "His massive arms are wrapped around you, protecting you. You can run under his covering of majesty and hide. His arms of faithfulness are a shield keeping you from harm." (TPT)

She had never read verse 2 that says that God alone is our refuge or that verse 9 says that He is our dwelling place. And yet, she knew all of this truth because Truth Himself told her. Olivia didn't know that the color of royalty used in scripture is purple, she only knew His voice. She heard the whisper of God and spoke it into our lives. The moment that began with concern and fear, God redeemed by chasing away that fear with His perfect love.

His perfect love calls us His own and makes our home in Him. God took the prayer I prayed for the revelation of Psalm 91, and He gave Olivia more than I even asked Him for. She still speaks out this truth that He declared directly to her. Our youngest daughter, Evre, who is four years old now, just asked me that exact same question. And the words that God spoke to Olivia that night 7 years ago, still sustain us now. God breathed life into Evre as I spoke those very same words again. The Bread that God spoke to Olivia that night years before, He also gave to Evre. Those words still carried His Presence into our family to bring a legacy of His protection and His arms around us . He is our house.

HIs words remain. His words still carry life. God has used those words, God is our house, for even more than our protection. As a family, we have moved cities and states a lot in a relatively short amount of time. Often, as a family, we just feel exhausted from what can feel like constant change in our lives. It's part of our journey, and it's beautiful, but we have felt the pull of just wanting to be "home." Jesus has gone ahead of us in all of these moves, and we've just been following Him as He leads. He has been faithful to go behind us and follow us with only His goodness. And in that, He has breathed life into us again and again, that He is our house. Even in the tension of changing houses, cities, and states, the revelation that He is our house has sustained us. He has brought life to us, perspective, and strengthened the bond of our family in those simple words He spoke to Olivia. Our family is always "home." He is our house.

Jesus lived that way. Jesus lived by every word that proceeded from the mouth of God. If one verse sums this up, it would be this verse which Jesus spoke of Himself, "I am able to do nothing of Myself [independently, of My own accord - but only as I am taught by God and as I get His orders]. EVEN AS I HEAR, I judge [I decide as I am bidden to decide. AS THE VOICE COMES TO ME, so I give decision], and My judgement is right (just, righteous), because I do not seek My own will [I have no desire to do what is pleasing to Myself, My own aim, My own purpose] but only the will and pleasure of the Father Who sent Me." John 5:30 (AMP) emphasis added.

Even as Jesus would hear the voice of God, He would do. This describes a fluid relationship... not stagnant. It describes a fresh, active, and immersive relationship. A conversation that doesn't end. He did nothing and said nothing unless He had first heard it from the Father. This is how we are to live. This is part of our inherent nature being alive in Christ. The intimacy with the Father that Jesus has, and that He walked in on this earth with, he shares with us. He shares this constant communication with Him. Jesus shares the Bread . He is the First to share this Bread, and He has asked me to freely give as I have freely received.

We have been brought into the family of God, and God designed us to hear His voice. Our inheritance gives us place in His arms and we hear His voice. It's who we are. Our daily bread depicts a life of hearing God daily and being aware of and abiding in the Presence of our Father, where He needs only whisper for us to hear Him . God is your house, too. In fact, I John 4:16 tells us, "All who declare that Jesus is the Son of God have God living in them, and they live in God" (NLT). The Message Translation says of that verse, "Everyone who confesses that Jesus is the God's Son participates continuously in an intimate relationship with God. We know it so well, we've embraced it heart and soul, this love that comes from God."

If we live our lives believing a lie that tells us God's voice is distant, elusive or unattainable, we will miss out on our daily sustenance that is meant to show us more of Who He is and who we are in Him.  Because of Jesus, there is no veil. Because of Jesus, there is no separation. Because of Jesus, Who is the Word, we are Spirit on spirit. Hearing the voice of God is not just a perk as a

The truth is that the
voice of God is the
most familiar voice you
know. It's the voice
that brought you into
creation and *it's this voice
that sustains you.*

child of God, it defines our being, our inheritance, our identity. Your identity is in the Word, Jesus. Hearing His voice is your life.

His voice is near. When we speak, our voice becomes audible as the vibrations from the air that we push out when we speak turn into the voice that we hear. And we were made in the image of our Father. He speaks, and we can also speak. Remember in Genesis that God created the world by speaking it into existence. God speaks. God has a voice. This is how all creation came into existence. With Jesus, the Word, God spoke.

A quick internet search of the smallest matter on earth will lead you to study the atom. Atoms were once thought to be indivisible, but as science and research have progressed, scientists have discovered that the atom can indeed be split. Inside atoms are protons, neutrons and electrons. And even within each of those are what scientists call, quarks. Quarks are made up of strings, and these strings vibrate. The foundation of all matter consists of vibrations.

Albert Einstein famously concluded, "Everything in life is vibration". Voice is vibration. So, as a child of God, if you take a moment to think of how God created the world and all that is within it, suddenly, these vibrations are more than just a scientific find. Everything in life is the voice of God. Science is unwrapping mysteries that have been lovingly placed by God to lead us to Him. And I'm sure by the time that you are reading this book, they will have discovered even more beyond what I've written here. Whatever way you examine the creation, inevitably it will lead you to the Creator. God created you with His Word, Jesus. You, your spirit, soul, and body are made of His voice. His voice is how you came into existence. The truth is that the voice of God is the most familiar voice you know. It's the voice that brought you into creation and it's this voice that sustains you.

When the people built the Tower of Babel, their goal was to reach to heaven. The continuing battle so many fought to get from earth to heaven. God would not allow it. He confused their languages so they could no longer work together. Communication is vital to building anything. They could not keep moving forward because Jesus had not yet come to give them access to heaven.

Quantum physicists are discovering that where we once thought all matter

———

He is the Beginning
and the End, and yet
He is infinite.

———

ended, is actually the point where a new dimension begins. And the more they press in and search out these new discoveries, the more they are finding that there is no other conclusion than that there is more that exists than previously thought. And that there is a realm that is unseen that we didn't know existed, yet holds within it all that we knew to exist.  New heights of innovation are being climbed to every day. True innovation always leads humanity heavenward. All that we know to exist is not just made of the finite, but the infinite. They are beginning to find Him. And God is not stopping them now. Actually, He's calling them. It's His voice that is leading us to His Presence. He is the Beginning and the End, and yet He is infinite.

> Throughout our history God has spoken to our ancestors
> by his prophets in many different ways. The revelation he
> gave them was only a fragment at a time, building one
> truth upon another. But to us living in these last days,
> God now speaks to us openly in the language of a Son,
> the appointed Heir of everything, for through him God
> created the panorama of all things and all time. Hebrews
> 1:1-2 (TPT)

Jesus is the language God speaks to us. Jesus, the Word, is our language with the Father. The language that needs no translation is Jesus, the Son. To get to the Father it would take one unified Language, the Son. After the days of Noah, the people of the earth all spoke the same language. This gave them a unique ability to work in unison. This unity culminated in the Tower of Babel. The people had worked together as a way to get from earth to heaven, and if had succeeded, they would have ended their journey with a devastating blow. They would have experienced the unholy trying to stand before He who is holy. It would not have ended well for them. And just like the Pharisees and Sadducees who would come after them, they were believing they could be their own savior and build their way from earth to heaven. So, God confused their language, and this formed a barrier between the people who instantly spoke different languages and knew no other language but their own. They could no longer work in unity. And the Tower of Babel failed., Well, it didn't so much fail, as God is His mercy held them back because He would send His Son from heaven to earth to save them.

All things that were made, all that we know to exist, are made of the

———

All things that were made, all that we know to exist, *are made of the vibrations of the voice of God* that still sustain our existence to this day.

———

vibrations of the voice of God that still sustain our existence to this day. His voice is not far, it's all around us, and in us. It's what we are made of. We are God-breathed words that are held together by the Word, Jesus. We are vibrating with the truth of who He is. And not only the children of God, but non-believers as well, can hear His voice. They too, are made of His voice. As a child of God, not only can we follow His presence and be face to face with Him and commune with Him, but for those who are still lost, it's His voice that will lead them to His presence.

When Jesus breathed His spirit in you at your moment of salvation, those vibrations, that you are made of, came alive and you found your rhythm in Jesus. The vibrations that make up all matter of your being now sing the same song that He sings over you. You are awake to reflect the Son because you were made in His image, and a new day has dawned in the light of His face.

There is a language that existed before time began. The vibrations science has discovered move in the Language of the Word . The Word that formed these vibrations still sustain them. There is no need to confuse languages anymore because there has been made a Way to the Father. This language would declare unity. This language would be the language that the world could be translated into to be one with God just as Jesus is one with Him. This is what Jesus prayed for you. (John 17) And that language is the language of the Son, Jesus. He is our union with the Father. .All of creation is made of Him and exists in Him, and the more people learn about the universe, the more they will see Jesus revealed. Science is searching for answers to the mysteries of the universe, and instead they are finding Jesus the Creator. Even man's search to disprove God, He will use to lead them to Christ.

The very voice of God, His Word spoken by Him to make all creation, vibrates and calls out who He is and who you are in Him. Science is discovering what has been in the Bible all along. With this in mind, let's look again at John 1:1-4.

> In the beginning [before all time] was the Word (Christ),
> and the Word was with God, and the Word was God
> Himself. He was present originally with God. All things
> were made and came into existence through Him; and

———

Hearing the voice of God *is who you are*. Hearing His voice is inherent to the life we live in Jesus.

———

without Him was not even one thing made that has come
into being. In Him was Life, and the Life was the Light of
men.

You are made of His voice. All of creation that we know to exist, and that which we have yet to discover, was made by Him and is sustained by Him. It's His Word, Jesus, and it's His voice that we know to be reality. All things consist in Jesus. His voice is here. We were absolutely made to hear His voice; we are literally made of His voice. We were created by and through the Word, Jesus. You are in Jesus, and in Jesus, you are in the Father. You exist, consist and remain in the Word of God that holds you. He sustains you. Hearing the voice of God is who you are. Hearing His voice is inherent to the life we live in Jesus.

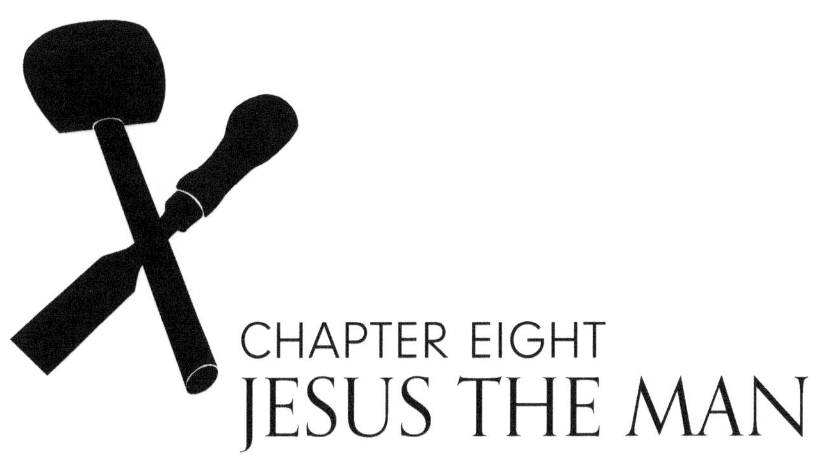

# CHAPTER EIGHT
# JESUS THE MAN

Seeing now that Jesus, being the Word, is our direct connection to the voice of our Father, in this chapter, we're going to look at how Jesus modeled for us this life of hearing the voice of God. There is so much to see in Colossians 1. I wanted to give you a portion of that chapter in the Bible so you can see and allow the Holy Spirit to bring more revelation to you and have His perspective as you read this chapter, but I encourage you to read through all of Colossians 1 in your Bible. After seeing all that we saw about the Word, Jesus, I believe you will see this chapter in Colossians with a new perspective.

> We look at the Son and see the God who cannot be seen. We look at this Son and see God's original purpose in everything created. **For everything, absolutely everything, above and below, visible and invisible, rank after rank after rank of angels - everything got started in Him and finds its purpose in Him. He was there before any of it came into existence and holds it all together right up to this moment.** And when it comes to the church, he organizes and **holds it together**, like a head does a body. He was supreme in the beginning

and - leading the resurrection parade - He is supreme in the end. From beginning to end He's there, towering far above everything, everyone. So spacious is He, so roomy, that everything of God finds its proper place in Him without crowding. **Not only that, but all the broken and dislocated pieces of the universe - people and things, animal and atoms - get properly fixed and fit together in vibrant harmonies, all because of His death, His blood that poured down from the cross.** You yourselves are a case study of what He does. At one time you all had your back turned to God, thinking rebellious thoughts of Him, giving Him trouble every chance you got. But now, by giving Himself completely at the Cross, actually dying for you, Christ brought you over to God's side and put your lives together, **whole and holy in His Presence**. You don't walk away from a gift like that! You stay grounded and steady in that bond of trust, constantly tuned in to the Message, careful not to be distracted or diverted. There is no other Message - just this one. Every creature under heaven gets this same Message. Colossians 1:15 -23 (MSG) emphasis added

Jesus holds us all together, even in this moment. God has been speaking this truth and He has given us a purpose. As we've discussed, we find our identity in Him. Our lives, being in Him, are put together as a relationship with the Father and His children, in the very relationship Jesus has with Him. We've seen that when God created Adam, that He gave Him more than just his existence, but that God also gave Adam his function, his purpose. Adam's purpose was to have dominion over the earth and to subdue it. Adam was given the position of partner with God to bring heaven to earth.

Jesus didn't come to change how the world was designed, He came to bring it back to its original design, through Himself. I love how my husband says it, "Jesus didn't come to turn the world upside down, He came to turn the world right side up." Jesus came to bring us back to the Father. The Word of God, Himself, came to rescue us, and bring us back. When we live in disconnect from Him, we are so far from who we were intended to be. The world has taken on a belief that who we really are, is a bunch of sinners with an origin of flesh. And in the church, we've believed that while we may be saved, we're still sinners, and still disconnected from God. That our first nature, what's natural to us, is the distance between God and man, instead of the nearness of the Father and Son.

These beliefs lead us to assume that hearing the voice of God is rare. It's difficult. We read the Bible stories of people hearing God's voice, and much like the Israelites, we say it's not for us. Maybe for Moses, but not for us. When we see ourselves, even as a believer, yet distant from God, and as saved yet still inherently a sinner, the voice of God is feared to be merely an outlet for Him to express his disappointment or anger towards us.

In Exodus, we read that the Israelites felt this way about the voice of God. Even after God had spared them from every plague of the Egyptians, had led them out through dry land in the midst of the sea, had wiped out their enemies, had given them manna and quail in the desert, gushed water from a rock, and even though they were told that God had chosen them to be His people, they lived in fear of hearing the voice of God.

When God met with Moses at Mount Sinai to give him the Ten Commandments in Exodus 20:18-19 (MSG), we read the response of the Israelites.

> All the people experiencing the thunder and lightning,
> the trumpet blast and the smoking mountain, were afraid
> - they pulled back and stood at a distance. They said to
> Moses, "You speak to us, and we'll listen, but don't have
> God speak to us or we'll die." Moses spoke to the people:
> "Don't be afraid. God has come to test you and instill a
> deep and reverent awe within you so that you won't sin."
> The people kept their distance while Moses approached
> the thick cloud where God was.

The Israelites were afraid of the voice of God. They kept their distance and they preferred for Moses to hear the voice of God. They assumed, or at least were willing to risk, that Moses would live, and they could just hear it from him instead.

I think that so often, when we look at the life of Jesus, we misunderstand His

———

Being seated with
Christ is not just some
metaphorical idea
to make being a
Christian sound better.
It's *our reality.*

———

relationship with the Father. We know He would hear and obey the voice of God. And we see what we assume to be an unattainable way of life- and a reputation of signs and wonders that Jesus performed in His own power. How many times have you thought to yourself, "Well, that was Jesus. Of course He left a trail of miracles behind Him. He's God. Yes, obviously Jesus could hear the voice of God, He's Jesus." And while it is completely true that He is God, it's also completely true that He became fully human as well.

We're going to discuss in greater detail the truth of Jesus laying down His deity to become human later on in this book, but for now, I want you to understand the truth that Jesus did not communicate with God in a way that was only reserved for Him. Jesus had to take on the boundaries of mankind in order to partner with God as a human to save us. He was fully God and fully Man. Because of that, just in the same way that He could live with the reality of heaven on earth, so can we. Being seated with Christ is not just some metaphorical idea to make being a Christian sound better. It's our reality.

When the Israelites assumed that God's voice was meant to punish, they became afraid. 1 John 4:18 describes that paradigm this way, "There is no fear in love [dread does not exist], but full-grown (complete, perfect) love turns fear out of doors and expels every trace of terror! **For fear brings with it the thought of punishment, and [so] he who is afraid has not reached the full maturity of love** [is not yet grown into love's complete perfection.] (AMP). Emphasis added.

The Israelites did not want to take part in that meeting between God and Moses at Mount Sinai. The Israelites wanted Moses to speak to God and hear from Him for them.

This paradigm has proved to be very costly. And this way of thinking originated in the Garden of Eden. Similarly, Adam and Eve became afraid of the presence of God. As we've discussed, the voice of God is in the presence of God.

When Adam and Eve sinned, they realized they were naked. They were operating from the position and perspective of having the knowledge of good and evil. The separation from God in their spirits had already taken place in the moment they sinned. When they heard the sound of God walking in the garden that evening, the Bible tells us they were afraid. Adam and Eve hid themselves because they were naked. They hid from God. They hid from the One that they had only ever known as love. Fear crept in because fear has to do with punishment. There was the feeling of separation and guilt in them. Their sin had separated them from God. Though their fear was strong, it never changed the love of God. In love, He took them out of the Garden of Eden where the Tree of Life stood. If they ate from this tree while in this separated state of death, they would live forever in separation from God. The mark of their sin could not be erased without a sacrifice. An exchange of death for life. Having this burden of sin caused them to fear the presence of God.

When we see ourselves as saved yet sinners, and children of God still separated by distance, we haven't rested in His perfect love for us. The Bible tells us to abide in His love. We have been given the privilege of resting in His love toward us. The sacrifice on the cross wiped away the mark of our sin and instead we have been marked as His own. The exchange of his death for our life has covered our sin with His blood. The risen blood of Jesus is the blood that flows through your veins. No longer to live in shame and fear of punishment, but to rest in His love and to rest in His presence. To hear His voice.

Just as the serpent deceived Eve into believing she had to attain something that she already had, so many believers have believed a lie that tells them they can't hear God. And when we don't listen because we are either afraid of His voice, or assume He's not speaking to us, we will never partner with Him with our words. That's what those lies are intended to do: to keep you from speaking what God is speaking, to keep you from realizing your true identity.

God's voice is not just for some, and it's not just for Jesus. You are made by and of His voice. His Word, Jesus, is who you are alive in. The Word is He who brought you into the intimate presence of the Father and clothed us with His righteousness. God has no punishment for you. All punishment for every sin was taken upon Jesus and Jesus left it in hell along with your every sin.

You are a child of God. There is no need to fear His voice because God, Who is love, calls you His own. There is no fear in love, and there is no punishment in His presence or His voice for you. There is no need to live distracted from the truth that says He holds you close and because He holds you close, He needs only to whisper for you to hear His voice. The truth is, your identity in Christ shows you how you are to hear and speak just as Jesus did. Seeing ourselves in the eyes of Jesus, we see that the way Jesus lived in direct communication with the Father is how we are to live.

Jesus tells us in John 5:30 (AMPC):

> I am able to do nothing from Myself [independently, of My own accord - but only as I am taught by God and as I get His orders]. Even as I hear, I judge [I decided as I am bidden to decide. **As the voice comes to Me**, so I give a decision], and My judgement is right (just, righteous) because I do not seek or consult My own will [I have no desire to do what is pleasing to Myself, My own aim, My own purpose] but only the will of the Father who sent Me.

Jesus said and did nothing apart from what God said. Jesus knew His identity. He knew that as a human, He had to partner with God. This is how Jesus lived. He lived enabled by God, empowered by the Holy Spirit, and Jesus enacted the voice of God in the power of His Spirit on this earth. Seeing ourselves in Jesus, we see that we are enabled by God and that we are to be empowered by the Holy Spirit to enact the will of God and bring heaven to earth.

I love how God gives us examples in creation to show us more of Himself. And by seeing more of Him, we see more of ourselves.

There are three parts to the process of voice in our bodies. There are three Persons in the Trinity - The Father, Son and the Holy Spirit. And being made in the image of God, there are three parts to us, spirit, soul, and body.

This text is from The American Academy of Otolaryngology - Head and Neck (www.entnet.org) and is an explanation of how the human voice is designed to create sound. Let's read this excerpt to see how the three parts of voice work in the human body.

> How the voice works - the power source is lungs, the

vibrator is the voice box the resonator is your throat,
nose, mouth and sinuses - the power of your voice comes
from air that you exhale. When you inhale, the diaphragm
lowers and the rib cage expands drawing air into the lungs.
As we exhale the process reverses and the air exits the
lungs, creating an airstream in the trachea. This airstream
provides the energy for the vocal folds in the voice box
to produce sound. the stronger the airstream, the stronger
the voice. give your voice good breath support to create a
steady strong airstream that helps you make clear sounds.

The voice box vibrates when we produce voice, the
airstream passes between the two vocal folds that have
come together. These folds are soft and are set into
vibration by the passing airstream.

the resonator- by themselves, the vocal folds produce
a noise that sounds like simple buzzing, much like the
mouthpiece of a trumpet. All of the structure above the
folds, including the throat, nose and mouth, are part of the
resonator system... the buzzing sound created by vocal
fold vibration is changed by the shape of the resonator
tract to produce our unique human sound.

When our voices are healthy, the three main parts work
in harmony to provide effortless voice during speech and
singing.

So, all of that to say, there is a picture of partnering with the voice of God
created in our bodies. As we read, the power of your voice comes from the
air that you inhaled and then exhaled.  Our power comes from God. He is
our Source. Jesus breathed His breath into us to receive His Spirit, and so the
air that we breathe, is His breath of life. The words that God speaks to you is
what you inhale, it's what you breathe.

In order for our lungs to inhale, our diaphragm must first lower and expand.
In order to receive the words that God is speaking to us, we need to humble
ourselves and recognize that the power and the words do not originate with
us. God is our Source. Any words that Jesus spoke on earth had to first be

spoken by God.

And then we must expand our hearts to receive what God is saying to us. We must allow our lungs to be filled and expanded with His breath so that what we breathe out is His word. We read that the greater the airstream, the greater the voice. Guard your heart. This is the part of our three-part being that determines our choices. Turn your heart towards His Spirit joined to yours and your ear to His voice.

The parable that Jesus gave us of the Sower and the Seed conveys this concept so well. Jesus talks about the Seed being the Word, sown by God, the Sower. The seed, the Word, has to start and come from Him. The different types of ground that Jesus refers to, are the different types of postures that our hearts can take when receiving the Word of God. But notice this, the seed is never different. The seeds never differ in quality. God will always give His best seed and His life-giving Word to you; it's how we receive the Word that determines if we will partner with Him in our true identity and function to enact it on this earth.

The parable in Matthew 13 of the seeds sown in the different soils speaks to the words of God and the hearts of mankind. The crops that were sown into good soil and yielded up to 100-fold the number of seed sown is a picture of words that are spoken by God to a person whose heart has been lowered and expanded by His Word. Another great picture of this is the two loaves and fish the little boy brought that Jesus multiplied into a lunch for thousands, including leftovers. You see, the Word that God gives you, that bread, is not meant for only your sustenance, but it is meant to be shared. As you share the words that God gives you and speak them into your life and the lives of others, God multiplies what you share.

Lastly, we see that the two vocal folds come together and that at that point of connection is where the vibrations are made. These vibrations flow to the resonator that produces our unique voice. This picture of partnership displays a coming together of two parts. They touch and then they create. The voice of God comes and touches our voice. Our partnership with God is Spirit on spirit. And His voice on our voice, empowered by the Holy Spirit Who moves and breathes over us, creates the vibrations that travel through to create the unique voice of partnership between God and man to bring

———

When we speak out
what the Father
is speaking to us, we
are *communicating His
Presence*. We are creating
an *atmosphere of freedom*.

———

heaven on earth.

We were not only designed to hear God's voice, but we were also designed to speak it out. This is the example that Jesus set for us. And this is the relationship that He won for us. Our partnership with God begins with Him and is sustained by Him. Jesus, who holds us together, gives us this identity to speak the Word of God. As Adam was to be the go-between with heaven and earth and to represent God, so we are now to be the conduit for which the words of God are to be spoken on this earth. But this partnership that we have with God is an even better relationship than what Adam had because we are found in Jesus . Jesus is our example. The life of Jesus flows in and through us. And by functioning in our identity, receiving and sharing His voice, the things on this earth that are incompatible with heaven become undone. And what is true in heaven becomes true on earth.

The Greek and Hebrew words for spirit are also the words for breath and wind. When we speak out what the Father is speaking to us, we are communicating His Presence. We are creating an atmosphere of freedom.

"For the Lord is the Spirit, and wherever the Spirit of the Lord is, there is freedom."
2 Corinthians 3:17 (NLT)

If we look at Jesus and consider ourselves in a different position on earth than He was, or rather is, we will miss the example He set for us. When we look at the partnership of three parts of the human voice, we see that there must be a source connection and sound produced and distributed. Our identity is in Jesus, therefore our position in this partnership is the very same position Jesus stood in. Our role is not to be our own source or our own power, but to be the mirror image of Jesus, who said whatever He heard the Father speak and did whatever He saw His Father do, being empowered by the Holy Spirit.

Sickness, disease, demons, the devil, winds and waves, and even death obeyed the commands of Jesus. And in His voice resonated every cell of His body. Jesus carried this authority, but not in His own power. He carried it by partnership with the Father. The power came in the authority of the Son of God, which is to say, His identity.

The anointing placed on His life was as a human, enabled and empowered by the Spirit of God. He took on the form of a human. As we just learned of our human voices, we must realize that this is how the voice of Jesus worked, too. He laid down His deity. He laid down His God voice and took on a human voice. He did this, so the partnership with God and man could be restored through Him. Jesus lived this, so that you and I could live this life, hearing and speaking God's voice.

Remember that Jesus said nothing unless He first heard it from the Father. The voice of God was with Jesus. And in fact, God placed His voice on the human voice of Jesus. When the disciples were afraid and thought for sure their boat would capsize resulting in their deaths, Jesus spoke. He spoke peace. He told the waves and the wind to be still. He spoke those words because God had spoken them to Him first. Jesus made it very clear throughout Scripture that He only did as the Father told Him. And when Jesus partnered His human with the voice of God, the wind and the waves were subdued. The wind and the waves recognized the voice of God that covered the voice of Jesus. When you speak what God says, your human voice is partnered with the voice of God. The power of His voice intertwines with your voice just as two vocal cords intertwine and wrap up into each other to create one sound. The circumstances on earth that are inferior to the reality of heaven will be subdued and in obedience to the voice of God. Jesus was fully God and fully Man. There was no struggle between the two. This was the way God intended it from the beginning.

A few years back, when we lived in Texas, I was driving the kids to gymnastics. The route we took to get there was a very familiar one. It was one of the few major streets that we could use from the newer neighborhood that we lived in, and so we drove on the street called 423 on a nearly daily basis. This particular afternoon, it was right at the time that all the kids were being let out of school for the day. The intersection we were coming up to was usually very busy, and it wasn't uncommon to see people riding on their bikes through the crosswalks from one side to the other. As we were stopped at the red light at the intersection of 423 and Panther Creek, I noticed a young girl, who looked to be around the age of 12, on her bike, waiting to cross from the left side of the street to the right. I was about 3 or 4 cars back from the stoplight, so I had a pretty good vantage point to see the situation that was about to unfold.

When I noticed this young girl on her bike, God spoke to me. He told me to pray for that girl's safety. So, I prayed a rather quick prayer and went right back to watching for that green light. About thirty seconds later, I saw this girl starting to ride her bike to the other side of the street. At first she starts out in front of the cars, but between the first lane closest to her and the fourth lane that was at the other side of the crosswalk and at the other side of the street, she starts to ride her bike in between the rows of the cars that were waiting for the green light. She rides her bike behind that first row of cars and is moving through the lanes going in front and behind these cars waiting for our green light. It's at this time, coming up behind me in that fourth lane, the last lane she needs to cross to safety, I see a huge white semi-truck. This truck is barreling toward the intersection. It was going so fast in such a small place and with so little distance between it and the crosswalk that it was obvious that this had become a very dangerous situation. And because this girl on her bike was weaving in between cars, it was also obvious that this truck driver didn't see her and she didn't see the truck. As I'm watching in horror at what looked to be an unavoidable and fatally tragic accident, this girl comes to the fourth and final lane with the truck rushing towards her. My heart stood still and I lost my breath. And then, by no less than a miracle, I look past the truck to the sidewalk on the other side, and I see the girl. She arrived safely on the other side of the street. It looked like she should have been hit but that somehow time was added or she was physically pushed to get her to safety in time. I sat there in amazement, and in that moment God whispered in my heart, "That's why I had you pray for her."

God's will was for that girl to live. His will was for her to make it safely across. He was speaking her safety into existence. And He asked me to partner with Him, to make what He said about her in heaven true on this earth. The circumstances that would have taken place apart from the voice of God, met the voice of God. His voice altered what we thought we knew to be reality and physics and made it heaven on earth. Jesus was there, and His voice is in His presence. Jesus, the Word, made what would have been true to that girl, untrue. Earth looked like heaven at that corner of 423.

You are called to bring heaven to earth. You are made to hear His voice and to speak His Word. This earth needs you to walk in your true identity. Jesus' perspective was from heaven to earth. He knew the way to cause earth to look like heaven was to declare what first came from heaven to Him and through Him to this earth. This is for you, too. Jesus lived as the point at which heaven and earth met. You have His Spirit inside of you. You are a point at which heaven and earth meet. Jesus told His disciples in Matthew 10:27, "What I whisper in your ear, shout from the rooftops."

What God whispered in my ear that day on 423, I spoke out. The authority I spoke in was not mine, but mine through Him. That situation recognized my voice because my voice was covered by His, intertwined and joined together as one.

His voice is in His presence. He whispers because He is near. When we prioritize His voice and His presence, and when we step into our true identity, our hearts will begin to look like His. And out of the abundance of the heart, the mouth speaks. Guard your heart. Decide who you will let influence your heart. Allow your lungs to lower and expand with His breath and His words will become your words. What God whispers in your ear, shout it out! The earth is groaning for you to be who you were created to be. What Jesus began in you, He is faithful to complete. You are anointed to hear the voice of God and to bring heaven to earth as you speak out the life and voice of God.

It can be easy to relegate hearing God's voice only to His response to questions we have asked Him. We give Him a question and we very clearly outline His multiple-choice options. We want God to take His pencil and fill in the bubble next to one of the multiple-choice answers we've laid out for Him. We feel like this is asking for what God is saying, but we have taken a false-footed start. Our approach is setting ourselves up to control the dialogue. We've accidentally tried to confine a limitless God to the only options we can see. Hearing God's voice is not about His response to us. Hearing God's voice is more about our response to Him.

God is gracious to meet us where we are, but it is an inferior goal to restrict what we are willing to hear God tell us. He knows what you need before you ask Him. And He sees the bigger picture. Very often, what we think needs to happen, or what we think is really going on, is just a glimpse, and there's something deeper than He can lead us into. It's not wrong to ask questions, we should be asking God questions. But, we have to also allow our hearts to be turned to whatever it is that God is communicating to us. Even when it seems to have nothing to do with what we want to talk about. A greater goal would be to turn our hearts towards HIs heart. Whatever frequency that His heart is beating to, would overwhelm our hearts and we would not only carry His words, but His heart. In this heart communication, we have transformation. Heaven is deposited into our hearts on earth. What He wants becomes what we want. We step into His identity and see ours.

God has used the many hours I spend in the car to continually show me this truth. When we first moved from Texas to Oklahoma, I quickly noticed that Oklahomans have a different set of rules that they like to drive by than what I knew to be normal. I noticed that my idea of when I should be let over or that my idea of when they should get themselves out of the entrance ramp lane and into the flow of traffic differed greatly from theirs. I spent the first few weeks getting angry just about every time I got in the car. In these moments, my girls got to witness the depths of my sarcasm as I proceeded to explain to the other drivers the error of their ways as they were busy driving by without even noticing me.

After more than a few of these incidents occurred, God started telling me each time to pray for that person that just showcased their misunderstanding of normal driving behavior. So, I received what God said, and I submitted and lowered my lungs to receive His breath, but I was still angry towards them. Then, I would start to pray for them, and as I would, my lungs, my heart, would expand. All of the sudden, I wasn't praying with a bad attitude, I was praying for these people with a fervency and a love for them that came directly from the heart of God. I first needed to submit my heart to receive His heart for them and, as I did, my prayers would go even deeper. I was praying His heart for them. I was praying His words over them. His voice came upon my voice, and I believe that those people's lives have been transformed because of those prayers.

What do you perceive in your life to be true that isn't true in heaven? What do you see to be incongruent on this earth with the truth of heaven? Jesus taught us to pray, "Your kingdom come, Your will be done, on earth as it is in heaven."

Jesus didn't pray carefully recited prayers. He prayed with fervency because He was praying the heart of the Father. Jesus was vulnerable with God. He

———

Jesus didn't pray
carefully recited prayers.
He prayed with fervency
because He was praying
the heart of the Father.

———

offered His whole being, His whole heart, will, and mind to the Father. He understood His position and the will of God to partner with man. He was always ready to inhale the breath of God and exhale that breath of life to the world. Jesus didn't use the same line every time He ministered to someone. He didn't have just one parable he taught. The Word of God is alive and active. Jesus said the very words that would cut to the core of each issue as God spoke those words to Him. Jesus even told us to not worry about figuring out what to say, because we are to submit our hearts to God, and He will speak through us. Jesus warned of prayers that were made of just mere words that came from the Pharisees and He charged us to pray with all vulnerability and trust. We have to listen to His voice. Prayer is not just us talking AT God. It's communion with Him. It's submitting our minds and hearts to the heart of God and the mind of Christ. Offering Him ours for His.

> For as the rain and the snow come down from heaven and
> do not return there but water the earth, making it bring
> forth and sprout, giving seed to the sower and bread to the
> eater, so shall my word be that goes out from my mouth;
> it shall not return to me empty, but it shall accomplish that
> which I purpose, and shall succeed in the thing for which I
> sent it. Isaiah 55:10-11 (NKJV)

Could it be that the word of God does not return void because we return His word like an echo back to Him? And as the word goes from heaven to earth, we partner with Him to bring heaven to earth? The word that is echoed back, working within the design of God with man, we see His will carried out on this earth?

James 5:16 talks about the fervent prayer of a righteous man. I was studying this verse once in preparation for a small group that I was leading. As I studied that verse along with some other verses, God pointed out to me the words, righteous and banner. Verse after verse, God was reminding me that when we walk in the righteousness that is the righteousness of Jesus, that we are living with our hearts, our wills, and our lives submitted to Him. Jesus freely shares His righteousness and His communion with the Father with us. And out of that communion comes intimacy in His presence. In that intimacy, God will cause your heart to look like His. He will cause His desires to be your desires. What His heart is fervent for, you will be fervent for. And when we pray those fervent prayers, when we partner with Him out of communion and a submitted heart, we are lifting up the banner of God's Word. This banner is the standard of heaven. We are speaking out into the atmosphere His heart, His will, and His words. And that's why those fervent prayers that are birthed out of communion with Him are so effective. As James 5 says, those prayers make tremendous power available. Those words are the very words God has spoken to you from heaven. You bring heaven to earth when your words are God's words. You pray powerful prayers when you first submit your heart to Him in vulnerability and rest, listen to His voice, and speak what He says. His Spirit on your spirit and His voice on your voice is heaven on earth.

One of the ways that Jesus explained hearing the voice of God, was through the illustration of the sheep and shepherd. Jesus tells us in John 10:4 AMPC, "When he, (the shepherd) has brought his own sheep outside, he walks on before them, and the sheep follow him because they know his voice." Jesus explains that He is the Good Shepherd. He is the One who leads us, who calls us each by name. And we follow His voice, and in fact, the voice of the stranger we will not follow.

As was commonly known in the day that Jesus spoke this parable, sheep would follow the shepherd. But, how much more so would they follow a good shepherd? As I was reading these verses about sheep, God showed me that these sheep that Jesus was referring to were sheep that not only followed the shepherd's voice, but they also prized the voice of the shepherd. The voice of the shepherd is so vital in a sheep's life that a good shepherd will make sure that he is there at the birth of each lamb so that their voice is the first voice the lambs hear. When God spoke to me years ago that His word was enough, He was teaching me to prize His voice just as sheep prizes the voice of its shepherd. Even with so many people telling us that we were crazy for moving to a new city where we didn't know anyone, that as long as God had said to do it, that His word was enough. We prized His voice above any other voice.

These sheep were expectant of the shepherd's voice. The shepherd's voice was in his presence. And in the presence of the shepherd, what they prized most, sheep were known to be at peace. They would cease from striving and they would rest. Their every need was met by their shepherd.

———

# What He whispers, we *will shout!*

———

King David knew the faithfulness of God, and he also knew the life of a shepherd with his sheep. David describes it this way in Psalm 23:1-6 (AMPC) "The Lord is my Shepherd [to feed, guide and shield me], I shall not lack. He makes me lie down in [fresh, tender] green pastures; He leads me beside the still and restful waters. He refreshes and restores my life, He leads me in the paths of righteousness [uprightness and right standing with Him - not for my earning it, but] for His name's sake... Surely or only goodness will follow me all the days of my life, and through the length of my days the house of the Lord [and His presence] shall be my dwelling place. "

God's presence is not to be prized because of what you think you will get out of it. His presence is to be prized because your heart is connected to His heart. This is your life blood. The resurrected body of Jesus is the body you partake of, it's the body you abide in as a believer. His body is the body you've been raised to a new life in and it's how you are now in the family of God. Even better than a sheep fold is a family. And even better than your average shepherd is the Good Shepherd. Jesus tells us, "I am the Good Shepherd. The Good Shepherd risks and lays down His own life for the sheep." John 10:11 (AMPC )j

We follow His Presence and listen to His voice. Jesus lived, died, and rose again for you to be near Him. You are meant to be living in His presence, alive in His voice. He is near. You are His and He calls you by name. Let Him tell you who you are. He will give you His heart. He will sustain you with His Word. Breathe in His Word and breathe out His will. He will lead, and you will follow.

Being found in Him, we see our identity in Him. As Jesus partnered with God, and spoke only what the Father spoke, so are we. As Jesus heard and spoke, so are we. As Jesus spoke with the voice of God anointing His voice, so are we positioned to do. What He whispers, we will shout!

"In this [union and communion with Him] love is brought to completion and attains perfection with us, that we may have confidence for the day of judgment [with assurance and boldness to face Him], because as He is, so are we in this world." 1 John 4:17 (AMP).

# CHAPTER NINE
# JESUS
# THE VICTORIOUS

At 27 years old, I had been married for five years and was the mother of a
2-year-old and a newborn. I was active in my church, as I had always been
from the time I was a young teenager, and committed to following Jesus
in every step of life. We had the typical struggles of a young couple with
kids. We had what felt like a constant uphill battle financially as we juggled
to manage a mortgage on our first home, groceries, diapers, cars, and our
first (and worst) endeavor at financial investing. We also had relational issues
within both sides of our families that took a toll on us emotionally.

Our marriage, even though good by many standards, was far from great.
And within the ebb and flow of good and bad circumstances, an emotional
storm was brewing in Ryan. His understanding of emotional health was far
from that of Heaven's. And in these early years of marriage and parenting,
our hearts were feeling a little more shattered every day with each new
argument between us. I held on to the fact that we were in this marriage for
life and in all the messiness, we always viewed the other as our closest friend
and confidant, yet for me, my love for him was fading after years of hurt and
disappointment. Though he never acted in the typical ways that we associate
with selfishness, he was definitely living out of self-defense and survival. His
emotions and goals to be the best husband and father that he could be were

wrapped up in his own hurt and emotional trauma from childhood. His learned defense mechanisms that he claimed as security from the time of childhood were the greatest threats to him. What he thought would act as his protection would become the weapons that would knock him down. Ryan had decided as a young child that he would keep himself on a path of perfection guided by his intense fear of failure. He would form preemptive guilt trips in order to keep himself on this straight and narrow path. Although fear and guilt can be powerful motivators for many people, they will ultimately lead you to irrational and unsustainable methods. This caused so much disconnection between the two of us. We would try to work out what we thought the problem was, but it never seemed to resolve anything. We were focusing on the symptoms rather than the root of the tension and disconnection. Much like I did, Ryan created a paradigm in which he acted as his own source and relied on his own power to control everything in his life. We may have tried different methods, but the mistake was the same. We were trying to be our own savior.

His journey of inner healing has been miraculous. To see him now, he radiates Jesus unlike any other man I've ever known. His humility and integrity are key components of who he is now. His selflessness seems boundless. One could say that He is a completely different person now than he was when I married him. And while that sentiment is not lost on me, that statement would be false. Ryan is the same man that I married at 22. He's the same man that would fall into childish tantrums when we were dating, acting with complete disregard for my feelings in our young marriage. He was still the same person. His identity never changed from the time God created him, but now he has found his identity . He has allowed God to work in him, show him the lies he believed, and he has taken hold of the Truth God has spoken to him that has set him free. And because of that, who he was always created to be is now, not only evident to everyone around him, but also clear to himself. And that is the game changer: knowing his identity and what God says about him. Ryan walked through the inner healing to look up and see what Jesus had already done for him. But, he wasn't the only one hitting emotional walls and having an identity crisis. At 27, I had no idea that I was barreling toward a breakdown. I was headed into a battle that I didn't even know existed.

In the fall of 2010, I spent the days and nights learning how to be the mother of two young children. That August, Olivia was born after a very difficult pregnancy and an even more difficult birth. I had to be induced with her at 37 weeks due to a failing blood platelet count that they detected after a high blood pressure reading. Your blood platelets aren't something you usually hear much about, but they are responsible for making sure that your blood clots enough so that you don't lose too much blood. With excessively low blood platelet counts, the fear is that the patient would bleed out. Some women experience low blood platelet counts in their third trimester. This is one of the reasons that many women would die in childbirth before the world had the means of detecting the issue. There is medication that has a small chance of working to help bring up your platelet count, but more often than not, the remedy is to deliver the baby as early as safely possible to avoid the lowest platelet counts.

My platelet count was so low that they immediately started me on Pitocin to induce labor. And I was given the news that, with the count as low as it was, I would be unable to have an epidural due to the risk of me bleeding out from having the small tube in my back to deliver the pain numbing medication. At first, it didn't seem like such awful news because I had always wanted to know what it would be like to have a natural birth. I had an epidural with Ava, but I really felt like I could handle the pain of natural childbirth. But the thing about a truly natural childbirth, is that you would go into labor naturally. A natural childbirth means that, at the time that your body decided it was best to deliver your baby, contractions would naturally begin, and your body could respond appropriately to the discomfort. But, this delivery was far from natural.

Even though I was 37 weeks pregnant, my baby would still be considered a preemie because anything before 38 weeks was considered early. My body did not naturally want to go into labor. And my body was being pretty stubborn. It took 2 days, 2 separate inductions, and the doctor breaking my water before my body would go into full labor. The insanely high levels of Pitocin being pumped through my IV made my contractions almost constant for hours and hours. And, Pitocin induced contractions are not like naturally induced contractions. The pain and sheer lack of relief between contractions was torturous. After two days of labor, I was writhing in pain and without any way to relieve it.

My doctor was running out of options and the nurses could hardly stand to see me at these levels of pain. Ryan and my sister were in the labor and delivery room with me, and they both looked at me with such disbelief as to how I could keep suffering through the pain and with almost no progression in labor. After 2 days, I was only 5 cm and the nurse finally stepped in with a suggestion. She suggested that I take medication that would help me to relax so that I could sleep in between contractions. My contractions would last 90 seconds and then I'd have 30 seconds to breathe in preparation for the next one. The nurse likened the effect of the medication to feeling a bit "tipsy." After I repeatedly turned down her offer of the medication because I didn't want it to get into my baby's system, Ryan and my sister started to plead the nurse's sentiments. I asked her if there was any chance it could harm the baby and she said that the only way it could harm her would be if she were to be delivered within the first hour of me taking the medication, but she insisted that with how slow my labor had been progressing over two days and only being dilated to five centimeters, she guessed that I was hours and hours away from delivery, so I reluctantly agreed. And in about 45 minutes, I looked over at the nurse and said, "She's coming! I have to push!"

The doctor was rushed into my room. Within minutes, they had a team of about 15 people there ready to save Olivia's life if she couldn't breathe or she was unresponsive at birth due to the medication that I had taken. The medication that I was assured would not hurt my baby, had now turned into a life-threatening emergency. There was no way to stop delivery. My body had finally succumbed to labor. Ryan and my sister stood there in fervent prayer for Olivia. Everyone, spiritually and physically, stood in a battle stance to save her. Within a few minutes of pushing, Olivia was born alert, crying, and in perfect health.

Thankfulness, relief, exhaustion, and hormones were met with more news that because of the dangerously low levels of platelets in my blood, I would need to stay a few days in the hospital for tests and to meet with a specialist just in case there was something more serious happening with my body. Newborn time is always intense. But, this time was particularly overwhelming. I hadn't seen Ava in days and, when she was finally able to come up to the hospital, she had to leave without me because I had to stay there with Olivia while doctors and nurses tried to figure out what was going on with my blood. After a couple more days, and what seemed like countless blood draws, I was cleared to go home having only to assume that the blood disorder was specific to pregnancy. I went home and began the journey of motherhood with two.

The first few weeks, I hardly slept as all.  As soon as I would get Olivia fed, diaper changed, and sleeping, Ava would wake up and I literally spent all night every night, awake and switching between both girls. When one would fall asleep, the other would wake up. Ava had been sleeping through the night since she was 8-weeks old, but she had just spent five nights in a row away from me when I was in the hospital, and she had never spent more than an hour away from me before that. And she could sense the adjustment in the house with our newborn schedule happening and the inherent changes to our family dynamic. It gave her a sense of uneasiness that kept her from sleeping well at night

Exhaustion was an understatement for me. And I didn't know it, but I was at my breaking point. As we sat down to dinner from a local market one night, I bit into a piece of chicken that shattered my world. I realize how ridiculous that sounds. Chicken. Just chicken. Well, not just chicken, I had eaten several bites of a piece of chicken that I found in the center to be the worst possible color chicken can be... pink! Salmonella! All I could think was that salmonella was surely coursing through me and into my milk supply. And if that were the case, I would be a threat to my newborn daughter. Every single question was racing through my mind. Is it possible to transmit that to my daughter through breast milk? How soon could I know if I've eaten chicken with salmonella. What could this do to my daughter? Why me? What are the odds? What am I going to do?

I realize this sounds a little dramatic over a piece of undercooked chicken, but I had blown way past reasoning and all the way into hysteria. I was sleep deprived, recovering from an excruciating and scary labor and delivery, and though unaware, I had been exhausted from so many other things happening in my life up until that point, that I was far beyond rational thinking.

The fear took over. I called the emergency room to find out what I needed to do. They didn't have too many answers for me. Probably because there wasn't much to be concerned about, but in my mind, it was" threat level midnight." I stopped nursing Olivia for 2 weeks and switched to formula just in case my body needed to rid itself of any remnants of salmonella. I never did get sick or have any symptoms of food poisoning, but like I said, I was way past the point of rational thinking. In my mind, I was a danger to my child. The very sustenance that was made to give her the vital nutrients that she needed felt more like a poison to me.

The fear of hurting my child took over. Even once I had made it out of my self-imposed waiting period and started nursing her again, I was terrified that I would do something to hurt her or Ava. Not through violence or anything premeditated, but by not being careful enough with anything having to do with germs or bacteria. It was the perfect threat because this threat was invisible. My imagination was the fuel that added to the fire of exhaustion. Suddenly, no surface in my home was clean enough. Every person and object seemed like one huge risk of making my children sick. And that was just in my home. Bringing them to any public place or touching anything that someone else had touched seemed like I was being reckless with their health. Everything that the girls came in contact with had to be sanitized. And I would spend hours, or even days, worrying about something if I felt I hadn't been careful enough. I went to the most extreme measures of sanitation and limiting what my kids could do in fear of germs. I held myself to the most unsustainable standards of cleaning and prevention that were not only unnecessary but debilitating. The smallest concern over the sleeve of my shirt touching a box of cereal while shopping for groceries would leave me wondering what or who else could have touched that box at the store, or even at the manufacturing plant. I would begin to wonder if Ava or Olivia had touched that potentially contaminated patch on my sleeve, and that would send me into a tailspin of fear. All I had the capacity for was to make sure that my kids were fed and taken care of while I fell apart. Ryan had to do everything for me. Any chance that I would touch anything other than the few spots in my home that I thought were clean enough would be too much for me. So, that was all I did. When I did start to sleep again, I would wake every day with a sense of dread. The fear had taken over my life. I didn't even have enough reasoning to allow myself to see that I had fallen into a deep depression.

My sense of identity was so far from the truth. I'm not sure that I had ever thought much about my identity. At that point in my life, I would have probably assigned identity to the choices you make or maybe your personality type. I think I always had the sense that my internal struggle was to become someone I wasn't naturally inclined to be.  Growing up, I was constantly told that I was too much or too little. If I disagreed with something, I was told that I was difficult. If I asked why or took a risk, I was told I was out of line. It seemed that at every turn, I was misunderstood and told to fear who I was and what I wanted to do. I grew up thinking I was always wrong. I hadn't recognized it when I was young, but I had been trained to be afraid of myself. And part of my training was that in order to overcome what was too much or too little about me, I would have to accept that I was hard wired for rebellion and fight like hell to behave as if I were not. I was taught to make my own identity out of the choices I made. As a result, I chose to adjust myself to present a picture of a person who could be tolerated and approved. My heart had always been in the right place; I never saw myself as a rebellious kid but if that was what I was told I was, I wanted to do everything in my power to do what I was told was right. I knew I had strong opinions and I knew I was very justice oriented, but that was never celebrated or discipled. Instead, I was reminded over and over that my conformity was priority and my strengths were problematic. So, in order to become who I was told I had to be, I would fight to prove I was good and lived by every rule and expectation that was demanded of me. The fear of making a mistake always hinged on the feeling of being inherently inadequate.

And here I was, again- afraid of myself. Afraid that because of my negligence, I would allow a germ to pass through the cracks of my carefully crafted sterile environment and harm my children. I was worried about things that even the most careful parents would never think twice about. I lived in a constant state of fear and dread. I was panicked and numb all at the same time. I would stare off and recount all that I had done, every miniscule detail, to see if I made a mistake in any way that could somehow lead to making one of my children sick.

The thought that kept torturing me was, *If I really loved my kids, I would fear for their lives at every moment and that fear would be their protection.* After months of this depression, whatever little breaks from the fear that I could grasp, were just long enough to finally acknowledge that I had to do something about it. And the only thing I knew to do was fight. I went after freedom and pursued it as if my life depended on it.

———

So, in order to become who I was told I had to be, I would *fight to prove I was good* and *lived by every rule and expectation that was demanded of me.* The fear of making a mistake always hinged on the feeling of being inherently inadequate.

———

I woke up with dread still, but I also woke each day to a goal. That goal was to rid myself of the fear and depression. My goal was to get over my fear of germs. Because that was all I could see at the time. There was something that was too much about me again and I needed to find balance. Being the good Christian that I was, I immediately set my sights on Satan.

Why the church has let this be a common theme in the Christian walk is beyond me. Why would we ever think that, in order to walk out of something awful, we should set our focus on the devil. Isn't that entirely contrary to the Bible? We paint a picture in our minds of little David going against the big, bad Goliath and we impose ourselves into the David character and the devil as Goliath. The problem with this picture is how we see ourselves. And, how we see the enemy. We imagine ourselves as the sure loser if God doesn't step in. And we envision the enemy as the obvious winner when going up against the likes of one of us little Christians.

Why do we assume we are coming from a place of smallness or weakness? Why do we assume the devil to be the larger and the more decorated warrior? We're not even correctly seeing who David really was. David was so sure of God's heart for him and His faithfulness toward him, that he didn't even see a need for armor going up against Goliath. And David definitely didn't see this epic battle as a lowly shepherd boy going up against a formidable foe. On the contrary, David declares how he had slayed the lion and the bear, and who was this Philistine to think He could go up against God? David saw himself as God saw him. He knew God was with Him. And when Goliath went out to destroy David, David knew it wasn't a battle of giant versus boy, it was a weak and feeble enemy going up against the Almighty God.

David had already been anointed as the King of Israel. David knew His identity. He knew his identity because He knew his God and He knew how God saw him. Goliath's size did not impress David because He had his sights set on God.

My immediate reaction to the fear and depression was to get in a battle stance against the enemy. I thought that something that awful could only be because the devil was forcing me into this dark place, and I would have to fight him to win back my sanity and peace. I was going to have to be really strong.

When did we ever see Jesus deal with Satan this way? When did we ever read of Jesus pumping iron to prepare himself for battle against the devil? It was actually just the opposite. When Jesus was led by the Holy Spirit into the wilderness for 40 days to be tempted by Satan, He rid himself of physical strength. He fasted for those 40 days and nights. He fasted before the devil showed up. He didn't fast out of a reaction to the enemy. He fasted in response to the Father.

Jesus didn't rely on strength and fighting , but rather this would all hinge on His identity and what He knew to be true about His Father. Jesus did not assume victory only once the devil left him. He knew He already had the victory that came with His birthright before the devil ever showed up. Jesus was of the Seed of God and one with His spirit from the beginning. He did not fear losing what already belonged to Him. The battle was not for the sake of obtaining a victory for Himself. This was to secure a victory that would be true for you. So, that you could rest in how God sees you and who God created you to be. Everything that Satan came against Jesus with was a lie about who Jesus is and a lie about who God is. Just as it was when the enemy came after Eve, and just like every time you have heard the enemy speak to you.

We assume that the way to defeat the enemy in our lives is to set our sights on the enemy, to shoot and kill. But, what you focus on is what you will order your life around. God's heart for us is not to order our lives around the enemy. And neither are we designed to order our lives around freedom.

I desired to be set free from depression and terror. I desired to be able to enjoy my life, enjoy my kids and my husband. I longed to feel comforted and find rest.

My plan was to pursue the enemy to take him down and pursue freedom. My plan, unknowingly, was to order my life around the enemy and freedom.

These things can sound so noble. Pursuing freedom... isn't that good? Aren't we supposed to have freedom? The answer is absolutely, yes. But our beliefs about freedom will determine how we relate to freedom. The pursuit of freedom, and even the pursuit of identity will never lead us to either of

———

When we look to Jesus as a mirror, we peer in and see the scars on His body. The scars from the nails and the whips that were lined with shards of bone,  metal, and even glass.

*Looking in, we see those scars that became His, were actually ours.*

———

those things. Our pursuit should always be Jesus. To pursue anything else is secondary. To find your identity, you will never look to yourself, only to Jesus. Even the pursuit of defeating the enemy, which sounds perhaps the noblest of all, would set our eyes away from the only One who gives us all of those things and more.

When we look to Jesus as a mirror, we peer in and see the scars on His body. The scars from nails and the whips that were lined with shards of bone, metal, and even glass. Looking in, we see those scars that became His, were actually ours. Outside of time, He took the wounds that you had yet to know. The healing of your soul is seen in His scars. Reach out and touch them, and let His healing turn your wounds to scars. We will fail to recognize the wholeness He has for us until we first recognize the wounds He took for us.

When Jesus died, He first descended to hell. He met with Satan. Satan had been holding the keys since Adam handed them over in the Garden. Man had given up his authority and dominion over the earth. Satan had the legal authority to wreak havoc of his own on the earth. Then Jesus showed up, fully God, but also fully Man. He was born of a woman, but of the Seed of God. This gave Jesus all authority on earth so that He could clothe Himself with our sin and die in our place. This is how we are able to clothe ourselves with His righteousness and sit next to Him in the heavenly places. This speaks to our identity. Jesus came with His identity as the Son of God, and because He had atoned for our sin, He could take possession of the keys and give man back the authority and dominion over the earth. And this time, we have the identity of Jesus that He shares with us.

The devil has already been defeated. Jesus has already won. Jesus is not asking you to go to hell and take back the keys because He already has. And He's given you the same power, authority, and Sonship that belongs to Him. As a born-again Child of God, He now shares all of that with you. Jesus is asking you to rest in Him. His identity, made inherently true about you with His blood, now runs in your veins and tells you your identity.

The devil has no more authority to use; he has been rendered powerless. His only chance to see evil on this earth is to convince someone who was designed to have dominion over the earth to hand over their power of free will. The degree to which you believe the enemy has access to your life is the degree to which you will give him access.

The truth is, the devil cannot take anything away from you without your consent. He is not coming from the place of victory to demolish us. He's actually coming from defeat and lying to you about it. He gives you the picture of an impressive warrior, when he is actually battered, beaten, and defenseless. It's only in bumming off your authority that he can succeed temporarily. We have to stop being impressed with the enemy and we have to stop seeing him as he wishes he was.

Your heart cannot spend all of its time pursuing the enemy, believing that this is a fight you could lose if you take your eyes off of the devil. This method only pulled me further down the spiral of depression and fear. Rather , you need to see the moment that Jesus took back those keys. Pursuing the enemy will only lead you to the enemy. I didn't experience victory from that dark season of depression until my sights were set on the eyes of Jesus. The eyes of Jesus show you His victory on the cross, the empty grave, and His love for you. The eyes of Jesus show you who He is, and in His eyes you find yourself. All that Jesus has, and all that He has won, He won for you. Your life is meant to be ordered around your Savior, in pursuit of His heart.

You are in a battle, it's just not the battle that you think it is. The battle is for your belief. Because belief equals partnership. When Jesus said it was finished, He shouted out, "TETELESTAI!" as He hung on the cross. Tetelestai translated to English is, "It is finished." The victory was won. The battle to win the victory was finished. The battle to make what was always true of Jesus true of us was won when Jesus shouted out that victory cry, "Tetelestai!" The cross was in the ground. The stake was in the ground. He had conquered it all.

I'm not sure we always recognize what part of the war we are in. When Jesus rose from the dead, He sent out his disciples to take what He had won for them and to distribute it to the world around them. The disciples were sent out and called apostles. The term "apostle" didn't start as a Christian word. The term originated in reference to war.  When a war was won, the winning entity would send out representatives as apostles. Their commission was to

———

The battle is not for your victory, because your victory has already been secured. The battle is *for your belief.*

———

take the culture and economy of the victorious region and make that true of the defeated region. Apostles were to infuse the culture that was inherently true of themselves to be true to those around them.

To call the disciples, "apostles," would clearly define to them where they were at in the war. The battle had been won.

Who we decide to partner with, good or bad, will determine how we live. Our belief is our commitment to partnership. We can believe and see what is already true about us, or we can believe we have yet to win and live with less than what is already ours. The degree to which you believe the devil has access, is the degree to which you will give him access. The battle is not for your victory, because your victory has already been secured. The battle is for your belief.

When we grasp that we are apostles, making true on earth what is already true in heaven, we can rest in the victory of Jesus that He won when he cried out, "Tetelestai!" for us. Instead of believing we have to war for our victory, our peace, our freedom, our healing, we can live in all that He won for us here and now. As an apostle, you can bring that healing, prosperity, peace and victory that is inherently true in you to the world around you that is waiting to hear, "tetelestai."

And what of freedom? How do I find freedom from the battle within? How do I find freedom from depression, anger, fear, doubt, anxiety, loneliness, bitterness, lies, heartache, and anything going on inside of me that is anything less than God's heart for me? The answer is not found in pursuing freedom. The answer is always found in His Presence.

"For the Lord is the Spirit, and wherever the Spirit of the Lord is, there is freedom."

2 Corinthians 3:17 (NLT)

"Now, the 'Lord' I'm referring to is the Holy Spirit, and wherever he is Lord, there is freedom." (TPT)

It's being in His Presence. It's not just what Jesus has saved us from, it's what He has saved us in to. It's knowing Him in a new way. Spirit to spirit. It's your identity. All that He is and all that He has is true of you. And it's not in pursuing freedom that we find it; it's in His Presence that we find freedom.

If we order our lives around freedom, we've made freedom our Lord. If we think we need freedom to be free, then we've assigned lordship to the idea of freedom rather than Freedom Himself.

Is Jesus the Lord over our hearts and the inner healing we need, or is it freedom? What will we set our sights on?

For so long, I tried to fix what was going on inside of me with fighting the devil and pursuing freedom, when what I needed all along was to bring to God all of the hurt and the soul wounds from my past that had festered and turned into a state of depression that was slowly but surely destroying me from the inside out. I had to bring the lies I believed about my identity and His into the light of HIs presence, where lies cannot stand, where His love casts out fear, and His victory rests in me. It was not about striving; it was about resting. It was not about obtaining; it was about discovering who He is and letting Him heal my heart.

You can confront the lies without assigning merit to the lies. We have to bring every thought into captivity to the obedience of Christ, just as 2 Corinthians explains. But, we have to do it with the perspective of heaven. Living under a lie  will obstruct our vision and the lie will look to be much bigger than it is. We need to come out from under the lies to see the greater reality. We need to look from heaven to earth and see the lie for what it is - a distraction. The lie is a perversion of the truth. The truth is never reactionary to the lie. The Truth came first and holds the greater reality. When all you see is the lie, you assume the lie to be the target, when the Truth is meant to be your target. When you look with God's perspective you see far more than your current circumstances. You begin to see there is so much more to what brought you to this moment, and God is wanting to bring you into total healing. If all you do is bring a thought into captivity, you may feel like you have asserted power, but that power is fleeting without the authority to validate that power. The authority comes in the identity of Christ and a captive thought is not fully dealt with until it also has come into the obedience of Christ. The lie must respond to the Truth.

For me, this looked like allowing God to bring the truth I needed rather than the truth I thought I needed. As I started to change my perspective from pursuing freedom to pursuing Jesus, I had to surrender my belief that I could figure it out on my own. I had to lay down my desire to find a scripture or truth to use in my own strength and knowledge, and instead allow God to tell me the Truth I needed in that moment. Of course, every rhema word from God will be congruent with scripture, but God was asking me to let Him lead me through and out of the darkness with what He chose to speak to me in each moment. I had to trust that He knew the root of why I believed the lies in the first place. I was going after solely the outcome I wanted, which was freedom, but God was going after my heart to heal what I didn't even know needed healing. The fears that I had been living in were only a byproduct of lies that I had believed long before. These lies had finally been expressed as postpartum depression. I had to surrender to God the way that I stepped out of depression, too.

Practically, that meant that I had to choose to only say and think what God said, even when what He said seemed irrelevant to the fear I was feeling or the problem I thought I was confronting. I wanted Him to say something that would directly contradict the lie I was feeling afraid of because I believed the lie to be the problem, but God wanted to bring healing in a much deeper way that would renew my mind to not only live in victory from depression, but to live in victory in all areas of my life. He was helping me to become more like Him. He was redeeming by belief.

If I brought a fear to God, and what He told me to say or believe didn't seem to address that fear specifically, I would choose to not give merit to that lie anymore by believing that was the problem. The problem was my belief, and I had to choose to believe what God said, even when it didn't make sense to me. I had to let go of being my own savior, and allow God to save me from those fears in His way.

Another practical way that I walked through healing was partnering with my husband. This was more than just a good idea; God told us to do this and because He spoke it, He gave us a tangible way to partner with Truth to work through the fear of that season and get to the other side. Every time I felt that debilitating fear over what I thought was a threat to my children's health, I would immediately tell Ryan what it was, and let him decide if it was a valid concern or not. More often than not, it wasn't valid at all. And if Ryan thought it was a lie, then I would choose to also believe it was a lie, and I would not assign any merit to the thought. I would choose to "throw it away" and move on. Even though this hit on every nerve of pride I had, having to check in with my husband all of the time, I knew that God had given us this way to actively engage in bringing every thought captive to the obedience of Christ. God gave me the gift of reason and wisdom through Ryan when the fear I was experiencing overshadowed my own reasoning and wisdom. This practical application of faith was blessed by the Presence of God because it came from Him. It was what I needed at that time. It only lasted for a season, but it was one of the single most important parts to coming out of the depression. It didn't work because of formula or method, it worked because it was what God spoke to us. His words not only carried the wisdom of what to do, but they also carried an anointing so that each time we engaged with what God spoke there was life and healing. I started to live in victory because I followed His Presence and listened to His voice. I fought by surrendering.

The battle is not for your victory. Satan most definitely does not have your victory. Jesus holds your victory and He's not keeping it from you. He freely gives it to you. The battle is for your belief.

In the books of Mark, Luke, and John we read of the moment that Jesus first appeared to His disciples after resurrection. The disciples were in fear for their lives, hiding from the Jewish people who had, just days before, shouted for the crucifixion of Jesus. The Man whom they had given their lives to serve, they were now desperate to disassociate from in public out of fear. They had locked the doors and shut themselves inside four walls of stone. Their hearts were heavy. Heavy as stone. They were enveloped by confusion. They went from seeing Jesus perform miracle after miracle to seeing Him suffer through the most excruciating death. They were locked in the walls of their heart with shame, guilt, anxiety, uncertainty of the future, and misery.

Peter had denied His Lord three times. The moment that Jesus looked at him, after his third denial, was surely weighing on Peter. The disciples' lives seemed to be heading towards one degree of glory to the next until all of the sudden it seemed to come crashing to a tragic end. Their lives looked nothing like they thought they would. The Man they thought would save them, they saw hanging on a cross. How could this be? After years of their belief in Jesus as the Son of God, doubt had barged in. Thomas is famous for it. He doubted the resurrection of Jesus. He doubted the validity of a Risen Savior. The disciples were questioning everything they had given their lives to and now seemed gone forever. As their senses were bombarded with every thought that screamed at them lies about their pasts and their futures, the only comfort they could find was a locked door and four walls of stone. These walls were their sense of security. It was a false sense of security, because the greatest threat was not the threat of losing their lives, it was the battle for their belief.

How often have we felt trapped behind four walls of stone in our souls? How many times have we felt surrounded and overwhelmed by our fear, doubt, shame, guilt, depression, anxiety, loneliness, and regret? We crouch behind these walls, desperate to break out. Desperate to save ourselves, desperate to break through these walls of thick stone that have entrapped us for so long. We can look at that locked door and trust that it will keep people out for our protection, but we look at those walls and wish we could break through. We ache to be free. We assume our only hope is to break through those walls. If Jesus truly is there, on the other side of those walls, we look at ourselves and the state of our hearts and try to muster the strength to get to Him. We believe that if we could just stop doubting in our hearts that we could get to Jesus. If we could somehow make penance for the wrong we've committed, then we could get to Him. But, we look at those walls of fear, guilt, shame, and depression and we see a stronghold that we could never break though on our own. We're trapped within our four walls of stone and a door that we have locked ourselves behind.

As the disciples sat in their disbelief and shame, the atmosphere in the room changed. The atmosphere changed but not because of the absence of their fear, but the Presence of Love Himself. They looked up, and they saw Jesus. Jesus came through the walls to get to them. He met them in their fear and their doubt. They never had to break through those walls to get to Jesus because Jesus broke through their walls to get to them. They only needed to look up.

His Presence melts away the shame and the guilt. When we see that Jesus is waiting there before us with His scarred hands stretched out towards us, we see the sacrifice that Jesus made and the resurrection power that has made you as alive as He is. No wall can keep Jesus from getting to you. You need only look up and see that He's been there before you all along. He holds out His nail-scarred hands to you to so you can see your own wounds.  He invites you to look in the eyes of your Savior and know His heart for you as His heart overwhelms yours and His healing Presence heals every wound of your soul.

Wounds do not speak our identity to us. Our scars do not speak of the wound, rather the Savior. Scars develop in our bodies by a process of white blood cells that come rushing to the wound site and cover the red blood cells with white blood cells. This is a much more detailed process than I'm saying, but in this most simple explanation, we see the goodness of God and the purity of the spotless Lamb's life covering ours. Putting His healing on our wounds.

There is a difference between a wound and a scar. A wound is something that we will often cover with a bandage and apply special measures of protection to, so as not to make the wound any worse. We sometimes even have to limit our movement and activity depending on the severity of a wound. In a small way, we will order our lives around a wound. We can surround ourselves with a false sense of security and a false identity that revolves around our trauma.

We assign value to whatever it is that we protect. And what we order our lives around, we worship. What we worship, we will allow to tell us our identity. So often, we let our wounds tell us our identity. A wound is anything that has hurt your soul and has been given license to alter your behavior and choice. A wound is not healed. It is actively a presence in your life.. A scar we don't have to protect or give preference to anymore. We don't have to avoid touching it or limit our activity. A scar doesn't have to be covered or treated. A scar is healed.. A scar is a testimony of Jesus. The scars on Jesus' hands and feet eternally speak to His testimony of saving you. And because Jesus shares His identity with you, His scars can become your scars. Your wounds can be healed and become a testimony to the goodness of God. His testimony can become ours. And we can order our lives around Him. This is worship.

It's not the pursuit of soul healing or of freedom that sets you free. It's the

Presence of God that Jesus came in to rescue you and bring you back into the Father's Presence with Him.

"For the Lord is the Spirit, and wherever the Spirit of the Lord is, there is freedom." 2 Corinthians 3:17 NLT

Knowing Jesus in this new way, Spirit to spirit, this deepest level of intimacy is where your identity resides. You overcome with who Jesus because He has made it true of who you are as well.  This is where we meet Him in His presence and our past, present, and future is met with the One who was, is, and is to come. He goes before you and only His goodness will follow you. That verse in Psalm 139 speaks to your soul and holds the shame and trauma of your past, the fear and depression of the present, and the anxiety and dread of lies about your future in His hands.  He holds you close to Him here and now where you feel His heartbeat in His chest as your heart follows in tempo. And He gives you hope for the future that He has gone ahead of you to secure. You need only to look up.

I got a call one day from one of my oldest and closest friends on a Sunday afternoon. We haven't lived in the same state in almost 20 years, but our relationship has stayed strong and grown despite the distance. We often have two, three, or even four-hour phone calls talking about all things from parenting to church to hilarious memories from our teenage years to deep spiritual and theological discussions. On this particular phone call, she had called to talk about a young woman that she has been mentoring. This young woman, Erika, is a new believer and has a heart to honor God. She's excited about her salvation, but she has struggled severely with her past. Her past is darker than most. She grew up with an abusive mother. She lived a homosexual lifestyle, she practiced cutting, and had regular encounters with demons. Before and after giving her life to Christ, she spent much of her time seeing into the spiritual realm where demons tormented her thoughts and heart.

Erika was doing the best she could to overcome the demonic following that plagued her. She had changed her behaviors. She went from trying to please the dark and the demonic to trying to please God. She wanted to live up to her name as a Christian. Her past told her that she was never good enough. In her efforts to reconcile the abuse and find approval she was desperate to do anything she could to make herself worthy of the love she longed for and to find freedom from the demonic spirits that she had come to find so familiar.  But the battle was not for the love of God or even freedom from evil. It was for her belief. This would not be resolved by what she could do from the outside to fix the inside. This freedom had to come from the inside, out. She believed lies about her identity. As my friend told me about Erika's past and her efforts now to free herself from the demonic and the evil habits that she had succumbed to so many times, God started to reveal to me what was really going on in Erika's heart. God gave me the word, *origin*.

God gave me a piece of His heart for her, and that love is what allowed the prophetic to flow into this phone call. I knew in my heart that the central lie that Erika was struggling with was that her primary identity was evil. She viewed her origin as having come from the demonic realm. She believed that those spirits who seemed so familiar to her were her default. The behaviors and patterns in her life that she lived out for all of those years in darkness, whether as a child who was victimized by an abusive mother, or a willing partner in evil practices as an adult, she had mistakenly identified that darkness as her original identity. And that belief will always lead you to believe that your default is darkness. It will lead you to believe that you have to be someone you were not created or designed to be to live in the light and that you're just one bad choice away from falling right back into the darkness. Instinctively, that lie would tell you that darkness is where you belong. No matter how evil and torturous it may be, the lie tries to convince you that the darkness is where you are most comfortable and most like yourself. That hell on earth for you is inevitable or where you fit best.

I told my friend what God was telling me about Erika's beliefs about her identity and a few other things that God had put on my heart for this young woman. We ended another marathon phone call, and both went back to our day and headed into the upcoming week. On Tuesday night, I got a text from my friend. Her text read:

Hey friend! So, Erika texted me at 6:30 this morning talking about killing herself. I was getting the kids ready for school and making lunches, getting myself ready for work... So, I responded with a combination of all we talked about the other day... Thank you for your Holy Spirit-inspired advice! Here's her text from just now:

Your origin is a pillar to your identity. When you know who you came from, *you know who you are.*

*What you said this morning about origin really changed the game for me today. I am really grateful. I had never considered the fact that I was born unto God and reborn to Him again. It has always felt more like I was reborn to Him and born unto the world... I definitely had never considered this.*

Origin matters. Your identity matters. What you believe about your creation matters because all creation points to its Creator.

"And by the blood of his cross, everything in heaven and earth is brought back to himself—back to its original intent, restored to innocence again!" Colossians 1:20 TPT

So often we relegate the story of creation and the simple truth of "God made me" to our preschool programs at church. The idea that this truth is basic and one-dimensional is so far from the truth. It is complex and revelatory and only to be understood with the mind of Christ, of which God has given us. Looking at this truth through the eyes of Jesus, we see an entirely different perspective. Your origin is a pillar to your identity. When you know who you came from, you know who you are.

You came from God. You carry a unique piece of the heart of God that no one else except for Jesus could ever carry. It's the Presence of God that awoke you to existence in your mother's womb. It was His voice that created you and His hands that knit you together to form your true identity. You didn't come from Satan. Redeeming humanity means to bring it back to who you originally came from and who you were created to be. Humanity was not created when Adam fell. Who you originally were was a God-breathed being, hand-crafted by your loving Father who gave you His image to bear and planned your every breath to inhale and exhale His life. His voice is the first voice you ever heard. And His Presence was all you had ever known before birth. The Kingdom of God belongs to children because children have the innate knowledge of God and sincerity of surrender and trust to the One who made them and called them by name. This is how we start. You may have walked away from that relationship when you were older, but your partnership with sin was never your original identity. You came from God and were made in His image. You came into this world as a child of God. Whether you walked away or stayed with Him, your origin is paramount to your identity. Your origin is Him.

"For the wickedness of humanity deliberately smothers the truth about God. In reality, the truth of God is known instinctively, for God has embedded this knowledge inside every human heart." Romans 1:18 - 19 (TPT)

God placed in your heart the knowledge of who He is when He formed you in the womb. Humanity came from God. And humanity was always designed to be its full and true expression in union with Jesus. The Bible was so carefully designed by God, that even the placement of the books of the Bible speak to this truth. Genesis and Revelation are the bookends of the Bible and, among many things, these bookends speak to our identity which is only found in Jesus.

In Genesis, we read of how God created us and that we do have an original design and that we are made in His image. The book of Revelation is a revelation of Jesus. Genesis declares who we came from and our original design, and Revelation reveals to us the only Way back to who God made us to be, and that Way is Jesus.

Humanity apart from God looks nothing like Him. In 2016, Microsoft launched an Artificial Intelligence (AI) experiment on Twitter. They created an AI chatbot named Tay with the persona of a young woman and gave it a Twitter account. Tweets can be a dangerous thing in the hands of humans, but it turned out to be much worse for a chatbot. Within 24 hours of the chatbot tweeting back and forth to other users and reading through comments on Twitter, the AI had to be shut down. Tay started tweeting comments that were full of hate and rage. They were completely vile. The problem was that a few human users decided to send Tay racist, misogynistic, and disgusting tweets in an effort to thwart the experiment. What Microsoft quickly discovered was that the AI was not programmed to decipher between right and wrong. And within only one day, the chatbot gravitated toward the hate for reasons unknown.

To quote C.S. Lewis' work *Mere Christianity* again, "Nothing in you that has not died will ever be raised from the dead. Look for yourself, and you will find in the long run only hatred, loneliness, despair, rage, ruin, and decay. But look for Christ and you will find Him, and with Him everything else thrown in."

AI is designed to act as if it were human. But, AI has an inherent flaw. Artificial

Intelligence is humanity apart from God. Therefore, it can never express humanity in its true sense. AI may be designed by man to display humanity, but humanity was not designed to be apart from God. Humanity's origin is God. Humanity is meant to look like God, reflect HIs Light, and carry His Presence.

> Throughout our history God has spoken to our ancestors by his prophets in many different ways. The revelation he gave them was only a fragment at a time, building one truth upon another. But to us living in these last days, God now speaks to us openly in the language of a Son, the appointed Heir of everything, for through him God created the panorama of all things and all time. The Son is the dazzling radiance of God's splendor, the exact expression of God's true nature—**his mirror image!** He holds the universe together and expands it by the mighty power of his spoken word. He accomplished for us the complete cleansing of sins, and then took his seat on the highest throne at the right hand] of the majestic One. Hebrews 1:1-3( TPT)

Like we talked about earlier in this book, Jesus did not save us so we could be God's people, but rather His children who live in His inheritance. He saved us to make us joint heirs with Him. He brought back the children of God whom He had chosen to be His own before the foundations of the world. After Eden was not plan B. The plan was always to have you as a member of the bloodline of Jesus. Jesus didn't save us to make us like Adam. Adam came from God, but He was one choice away from separation from God. When we accept Jesus' sacrifice to adopt us by blood, His very own blood, we are no longer on the verge of losing our salvation. We are now seated with Christ in the heavenlies, his blood coursing through our veins and our lineage taken from Adam to Christ. You have not been made to be like Adam. You were made to be like Jesus.

You have been redeemed to be in the Presence of God, where freedom resides and you find your identity. His Presence is where the trauma and pain that have crippled your heart fade in the light of His love for you. The agony in the heart of Jesus that shook throughout His body, as He sacrificed Himself for you, was the very agony that your heart has suffered. Jesus didn't just take the idea of your hurt and pain, He took your specific fear, doubt, guilt, shame, and your deepest soul wounds and endured the suffering for you. He was thinking of you. He was living through your abuse, your torment, your pain, your suffering. He was living it, holding on to it, so it could be nailed through His hands to the cross. His scarred hands reveal your pain, and they bring your healing. Your soul finds its healing in His presence.

When God breathed you into existence, you experienced His Presence for the first time. When Jesus breathed His Spirit into you, that is the moment of your salvation. In that upper room, Jesus looked at His disciples, breathed on them, and said "Receive my Spirit." That was the moment of their salvation. That was the moment where the blood that was shed just three days before was infused into their spirits and they became Children of God. This is what happened for you when you accepted Christ as your Savior and gave your life to Him. His Presence isn't just a fleeting moment, but it marks who you are, and He will forever reside with you.

Ava was around 8 years old when she told me about a conversation she had with God about love. The idea of performance and earning what you have isn't foreign to her. She is wired by God to understand the value of integrity and a good work ethic. There is inherent good in those things. But a lie can form if there is a twist at some point with what you believe that leads to the idea that you somehow have to earn love or salvation, or freedom, or anything else that Jesus freely gives us. Ava told me how God spoke something to her that totally changed the way she thought, and I knew it brought healing to her heart. He said to Ava, "I will never love you back!" It's just like God to speak to Ava in a way that seems so definitive and sharp, so matter-of-fact. Because that's the way that Ava thinks. That's how she speaks. God always knows exactly how to say something to us that meets us where we're at, but also meets us in the unique way that He created each one of us. Ava's bright eyes danced as she explained to me what God spoke to her in that moment. She said, "He will never love us back because He always loved us first!"

This revelation of the love of God continues to speak to Ava, and God continues to reveal His love to others through these words He gave Ava. At 12 years old, Ava wrote a song called, "You Loved Me First." It was a song she wrote out of this revelation that she stewards so well.. She entered the song in a contest at her youth group at the and won! They recorded her song and you can even listen to it on Spotify!" This song has reached so many and it all started with a word from God.

This is freedom! This is your identity. Your origin. His Presence, His heart, and His voice are the most familiar thing to you. You are made of His voice. The healing and freedom of your heart and soul will always be found in His Presence. You need only to look up into His eyes and let Him speak His heart over you. Healing is in nail-scarred hands. You can rest in those hands. You can rest in Him.

# CHAPTER TEN
# JESUS THE REDEEMER

"His blood be on us and on our children." Matthew 27:25 (ESV)

The angry crowds had gathered to ensure a guilty verdict from Pilate. They were there to guarantee the death penalty for Jesus. Pilate questioned Jesus but could find no fault in Him. Pilate's wife suffered a nightmare about Jesus and knew He was holy. She warned Pilate not to harm Him, furthering his resolve to release Jesus at this Passover. But he could not convince the crowd. In fact, the crowd was so vehement in their pleas for the crucifixion of Jesus that a riot was about to break out.

When Pilate realized that his efforts were useless, he had a basin of water brought out. In front of the bloodthirsty crowd, he washed his hands and then proclaimed, "I am innocent of the blood of this righteous man. The responsibility for his death is now yours.' And the people cried back, 'Let his blood be on us and on our children." Matthew 27:24-25 (TPT)

The cry for the blood of Jesus was made that day to take on the responsibility and guilt of the death of Jesus. They cried out to be forever marked by the murder of Jesus.

During a previous Passover, Jesus came to Jerusalem. As He went into the temple, He found the merchants and currency exchangers taking advantage of the people who had come to worship and make sacrifices to God. Jesus did not tolerate the exploitation of those who had come to worship His Father, and He drove them out immediately. The religious leaders questioned His authority to do this and wanted Him to prove His claim as the Son of God with a supernatural sign and Jesus responded, "After you've destroyed this temple, I will raise it up again in three days." John 2:19 (TPT). The religious leaders thought He was implying that he would rebuild the temple made by man, but Jesus was speaking of the temple made of God and Man.

Jesus was speaking of His body, the temple of the Holy Spirit, being raised to life again. His life belonged to His Father because He always chose the Father's will. Even before ever taking on the flesh of man, He was following the path of sacrifice to leave heaven to come to us.

"It was the precious blood of Christ, the sinless, spotless Lamb of God. God chose him as your ransom long before the world began, but now in these last days he has been revealed for your sake."

1 Peter 1:19-20 (NLT)

No man could take His life from Him. It was His to lay down. His body was His to give as a sacrifice for all. His blood was His to pour out. His spirit was His to suffer the separation of mankind as He hung on that cross and His Father turned away.

For the first and only time, Jesus experienced separation from His Father. This was the very reason Jesus came, sacrificing Himself to destroy the separation of the children from their Father. The blood of separation that was inherent in the seed of man, was being exchanged for the sinless blood of the Son. This is redemption. Jesus' blood was not taken from Him, rather it was given. Though He was innocent, His blood was poured out, and in doing so, His innocence is what made you faultless before God. This is redemption. The sacrifice that Jesus gave was His to make. The blood that the crowds pleaded to have on them and their children as a sign of their guilt to the execution of Jesus was actually the very blood that would be poured out for their forgiveness. This is redemption.

Their plea, their cry for the blood of Jesus, was not granted in the way they had demanded. Jesus prayed while being nailed to the cross, "Father, forgive them, they don't know what they're doing." Luke 23:34 (TPT). Jesus wasn't taken against His will. He laid His life down. The blood that the people cried out to mark their lives and the lives of their children was righteous. The blood of Jesus was not being poured out to make those covered in it to be guilty. He surrendered His life so that we could be saved. And the blood of Jesus was not on the people who cried out for His crucifixion because the blood of Jesus can only redeem.

The blood of Jesus doesn't mark blame. The blood of Jesus voids all offense and guilt. The blood of Jesus is what makes the forgiveness of our sins possible. His blood is what covers us and makes us a child of God, with a new lineage and a new bloodline. The blood of Jesus upon us is what makes us His own. This is redemption. Even the cry for the blood of Jesus has been redeemed.

There is no life that Jesus' blood cannot redeem. There is no circumstance, no situation, no person that His blood cannot transfuse. The crowds who cried out to Pilate for the blood of Jesus to be upon them, even that , He has redeemed. The very blood that they cried to mark their blame was the blood that would be poured out to save them.

Because now, all who cry for the blood of Jesus to be upon them become free of guilt, free of shame, free of sin, free of all bondage and slavery. Those who cry for the blood of Jesus are redeemed and free from the death of separation to God. They are free to be called His children. Those who confess that Jesus is Lord, and who believe in their hearts that Jesus died and rose again, have called out for the blood of Jesus. They have cried out for His blood to be on them, and they are saved. Jesus gave up everything for you. He literally went to hell and back for you. Now, you have the freedom to choose to surrender your life to Him. To call out for His blood to redeem you.

There is nothing so ugly that you could have ever done that the beauty of His blood cannot redeem. There is nothing so ugly that has been done to you that the beauty of Christ's blood cannot redeem. The innocent blood that was cried for on that Passover was bled for your guilt. Even the

_______

Even the cry for the
blood of Jesus
*has been redeemed.*

_______

bloodthirsty would be redeemed if they would only turn to Him.

What is in your past that seems so awful-as ugly as crucifying Christ and pleading the guilt of his murder on your children - that it feels as though it is unredeemable? What is in your life that overwhelms you with the feelings of guilt and hopelessness? What wrongs seem inescapable and cause you to feel trapped in shame and fear?

There is nothing that Jesus did not take with Him on that cross. There is no sin, no offense, that Jesus did not take the punishment for on the cross. There is not a moment in time that was not accounted for in the blood of Jesus. Jesus did not just take the idea of sin to the cross, He carried the very sin that you committed, but also the sins committed against you. When His blood was pouring out, His heart was turned toward you. The moments of trauma that haunt you to this day, that is what Jesus experienced as His blood was poured out. His blood was poured out for the abuse you suffered, the betrayal you endured, and the pain that crushed you. The nightmare you lived, He lived on the cross so that you could be free.

> He was despised and rejected by men, A Man of sorrows and pain and acquainted with grief; And like One from whom men hide their faces He was despised, and we did not appreciate His worth or esteem Him. But [in fact] He has borne our griefs, And He has carried our sorrows and pains; Yet we [ignorantly] assumed that He was stricken, Struck down by God and degraded and humiliated [by Him]. But He was wounded for our transgressions, He was crushed for our wickedness [our sin, our injustice, our wrongdoing]; The punishment [required] for our well-being fell on Him, And by His stripes (wounds) we are healed.
> Isaiah 53:3-5 (AMP)

His blood was poured out to redeem the sin you committed, the affair you chose, the abandonment you enforced, the lies you lived, the hurt you caused, the abortion you had, and every drop of guilt that tries to drown you. You need only to cry for the blood of Jesus to be on you. His blood will cover the guilt, shame, trauma, and the offense. There is nothing that His blood can't redeem. Cry out for His blood to redeem the ugliest parts of your life and drown the sins of your story in exchange for the story of the spotless Lamb.

Ask for His story, to now be your story. His story of redemption to become your story. His position as Son to be your position as a Child of God with the blood of Jesus transfused into all that you were, all that you are, and all that you will ever be. Cry for His blood. Because even the cry for the blood of Jesus has been redeemed.

Forgiveness is often misunderstood by the church. We recognize that Jesus forgave us of our sins, because that is central to the belief that you can be saved. And honestly, I think it's a very recognized aspect of salvation, because most people are painfully aware of the sins they have committed. We were guilty and yet forgiven. He was innocent, yet punished. This is the splendor of Christ's sacrifice.  But, what do we believe our forgiveness towards others actually means?  For many people, forgiveness is thought to be synonymous with acceptance and tolerance. The idea that forgiveness pardons someone's sin against us and frees the offender from punishment is often the belief many people hold. So, forgiveness can seem like the final and complete culmination of the injustice that assaulted us.

A few years ago, I was preparing a message to preach on forgiveness. The topic felt so heavy to me. I knew that the significance of this subject is so imperative to living in the truth of your identity and freedom. So, before I began, I asked the Lord what He wanted His Church to know about forgiveness. And He told me this...

I designed forgiveness for you. Forgiveness is meant to lift the burden of the offense off of you.

The forgiveness that Jesus freely gives us came at a very steep price. He didn't forgive us by ignoring the sin and defying justice. Jesus fully acknowledged our sin, which is how He took it upon Himself. Jesus knows your sin deeply because He experienced it as He paid for it on the cross. He experienced it in the most immersive way, from every angle of the offense. He lived in that moment taking on the broken identity of the sinner, the anguish of the victim, and the punishment for the crime. Yet, He did not deny justice. Justice was made by sacrifice. Punishment was given, but not to the one who committed the offense. This is forgiveness: Jesus lifted the offense off of us, off of both the sinner and the victim, and put it upon Himself. Punishment was given and justice was made by His sacrifice. He took your sin, but He also took on your trauma, your regret, and your pain.

The forgiveness that Jesus wants us to live in is possible because He carried the burden of the offense for us. The truth of what Jesus has done for us is what gives us the freedom to forgive. Because forgiveness is not to let the offender avoid justice or escape punishment. Forgiveness is for you. Forgiveness is for you to receive from Jesus, and freely give because of the forgiveness you have received. Forgiveness is part of the freedom and inheritance that you can only find in Jesus.

Forgiving someone has nothing to do with guilt, but everything to do with your inner healing. The forgiveness that God is asking of you is an invitation to rest. He is holding out His hands, waiting for you to put the offense in them. The offender still has to answer for their actions to God. That is between the offender and God. Forgiveness still keeps the offender responsible. You forgiving someone does not condone, diminish, or validate the wrong that was done to you. Rather, forgiveness releases your heart to live in freedom. It releases you from the offense that enslaved and brought upon you a burden that God never wanted you to bear. Unforgiveness causes you to assume responsibility for the sin or offense that was done to you and violated you. God wants you to see your pain in Him, so that you would see His freedom reflected back upon you.

Often, when we choose to not forgive someone, we ultimately are attempting to find some sense of control. Being victimized means someone asserted control and dominance over us. It was a false sense of control, but it caused great harm, nonetheless. As is unforgiveness... it gives us a false sense of control that only brings us more harm. When we choose to not forgive, we're not meaning to hold onto our inner wounds, what we're trying to accomplish is our dominance and judgment on someone else. This is reserved for God. And He is faithful, and He is just. We can have complete reliance on His judgment to be true. This does not mean we allow other people to assert themselves to our detriment. That ideology would lead us to the very thing that Jesus has set us free from. He has set us free from oppression. And any abusive relationship is not God's will for your life. Forgiveness means you maintain your self-control and what you will allow in your life. No one else can decide that for you. To believe that one person has power and control over another person requires a submission to the paradigm of fear, punishment, and control. That is not the paradigm of Heaven. When we remove the ideas of fear, punishment, and control, we find the fruit of the Holy Spirit: "love, joy, peace, patience, kindness, goodness, faithfulness, gentleness, and self-control. There is no law against these things!" Galatians 5:22-23 (NLT)  The Presence of God is where we find freedom. Because where the Spirit of the Lord is, there is freedom.

"Love never brings fear, for fear is always related to punishment. But love's perfection drives the fear of punishment far from our hearts." 1 John 4:18

Jesus has not saved you into a kingdom of fear, punishment, and control. He has saved you into His Kingdom. His kingdom is fueled by love out of choice. He chose you first, He loved you first. So we, because of His love, have also chosen Him. Love is not possible without freedom. Love is not love without choice. Jesus came to set the captives free. His invitation to you to live in wholeness and healing is wrapped in forgiveness.

Isaiah 53 tells us that Jesus took upon Himself our grief, our sorrow, and our pain when He went to the cross. He provided healing for your heart when He carried the burden of the offense for you. The forgiveness that you give when you forgive someone is the surrender that invites Jesus to lift the burden of the offense off of you and it is your first step into freedom.

Forgiveness lifts the burden of carrying the trauma, abuse, and offense off of you and allows you to live in the healing and freedom of Jesus. Forgiveness is you stepping into the freedom and inner healing that Jesus obtained for you. The burden of the offense is what weighs down our hearts and creates strongholds like stone walls in our hearts. Strongholds are any belief system that is in opposition to the Truth. Yet, these strongholds made of stone walls, Jesus walks through to meet you there in your pain. Even in unforgiveness, Jesus will meet you there. And if you will only look up, you will see His hands stretched out to you to lift the burden of the offense off of you if you will let Him.

This is where you can look up and choose to forgive. This is the moment that you can acknowledge the offense and bring it to Jesus, along with all the pain and the trauma and you put them into the hands of Jesus. That is the

———

Forgiveness lifts the burden of the offense off of you and allows you to move into your future in the *freedom Jesus has given you.*

———

forgiveness that Jesus asks of you to give. Because freely you have received. Freely you have received forgiveness and the inherent blood of Jesus to bring you back into the Presence of God, so freely you can give. You can trust Jesus that justice is alive and well in Him. Forgiveness is meant to bring your freedom. Forgiveness acknowledges Jesus' open hands to take your hurts and pains, because He already experienced them when He held them in His hands as they were nailed to the cross. Jesus loves you far too much to leave you to carry the burden of offense that you suffered. Forgiveness lifts the burden of the offense off of you and allows you to move into your future in the freedom Jesus has given you.

The storms that we face will howl with fierce winds and conjure up waves that come crashing down on our souls. Bombarding us from every side, presenting a sky full of darkness that seems to envelope us. We feel surrounded by fear and stalked by terror. Jesus didn't just speak peace to the storm. He is peace. His voice is in His Presence. Look up and see His hands stretched out to you. When Jesus was walking on the water, Peter called out to Him. And Jesus said, "Come." Jesus is inviting you to step out in the winds and waves that are shrouded in the darkest skies of the pains of our hearts and the wounds of our souls.

The winds and the waves, the darkness, seem so ominous. But when Peter looked at Jesus, standing on the water, He knew he could stand, too. He knew that if Jesus said, "Come" that His invitation was all he needed to jump out of the boat. It wasn't until Peter took his eyes off of Jesus and looked to the waves that he started to sink. The waves were there in his first steps out of the boat and onto the water. Peter was standing on the water, just as Jesus was. Those waves were there while Peter stood, but they weren't knocking him down. The waves could only pose a threat when he took his eyes off of Jesus and allowed himself to be overwhelmed with the waves. He chose to look into the waves of fear instead of looking into the eyes of His Savior. His fear was no match for the confidence and love that came from Jesus inviting him into His presence. The battle is for your belief. Peter's belief that the waves could knock him down and even sink him was the only reason he lost his footing on the water.

The enemy wants you to believe those waves and those stone walls are too great for you to break through to get to Jesus. The lie is that you have to break down anything to get to Jesus. As Peter looked up and saw the hands of Jesus reaching out to him in all of his fear and doubt, he saw that all he needed to do was to take the hands of Jesus.

Look up. Jesus is standing before you, ready to take every pain of your heart and heal every wound that lets the waves crash upon it and the walls isolate it in the dark. He is speaking truth every lie that speaks to you about who you are, who God is, and every lie about your past, present, and future. Jesus is offering you His freedom, to walk you through the pain and into His healing. We have to let His light shine on those dark places in our hearts that surround the hurt that makes us feel like we're sinking. We have to look up and see that the walls that once seemed impenetrable and the waves that seemed insurmountable have already been met by the Presence of the One who goes before us and whose goodness follows us. His words that wash over you and break down your walls are the truth that sets you free. What He speaks to you dispels the lies of the walls and waves. He is standing in front of you with His hands stretched out. You need only look up.

# CHAPTER ELEVEN
# JESUS THE SINLESS

As a culture, we have spent so much energy on labeling people according to their behavior and beliefs. These labels that we assign are not meant to lead you to your true identity, they are designed to give you your identity. But labels are not the image that you were made in, and ultimately will limit you. Personality tests, while useful in some ways, are not finding your identity, they are finding patterns of behavior and belief. Of course, that's not the language that we use, but it is the projection we subtly imply. Another way that we have assigned identities to ourselves is through focusing on what are popularly referred to as triggers. A trigger can be anything that brings about a strong, emotional reaction or behavior and is most often associated with past traumas. Identifying triggers can be useful to illuminate parts of our hearts and souls that need healing. And that healing is a process that Jesus wants to walk you through. Your emotional wounds and soul traumas are places in your heart that Jesus wants to meet you in to walk you through to healing and redemption. You cannot give to Him what you're not willing to acknowledge. Triggers alert us to recognize that there are deeper issues that need to be resolved. Jesus goes before you and only His goodness will follow you. Jesus wants to cover your past hurts, rejections, and pain with His goodness so that when you look back, instead of being triggered, you will be healed and set free to see His goodness and redemption.

The problem with triggers  is when we assign them as part of our identity. Becoming aware of your triggers is vital for self-awareness but this is a starting point, not a destination. Triggers are not the problems themselves. They can actually help you to identify a place in your heart and life that needs healing, but they do not define you. Triggers are never meant to tell you who you are; the trap is when we assume identity from them. The problem with triggers is allowing them to determine the paths we will take in our lives. Triggers do not inherently have the power to control our lives, they have to be given the power to do so. We have to give away our power of free will over to the triggers. So often, triggers and temptations or tendencies are seen as part of who we are. And they are used as a road map for how to navigate life by way of what to avoid.

We consider our triggers responsible for our emotional spirals, our rage, our alcoholism, our porn addictions, or our cycles of self-punishment. And the list goes on. We have believed a lie that these tendencies have been birthed out of a belief that who we are is revealed in our triggers. The truth is that triggers reveal our wounds and, at that point, we can choose to bring them to the feet of Jesus for His healing and redemption so that we can move forward in healing.

There are two schools of thought on how to deal with triggers and temptations. One says to order your life around your triggers and temptations as a way to avoid them. The other is to lean into your temptations because that is how you find true freedom and identity. Let's talk first about that first idea. For many people, particularly Christians, triggers and temptations are a huge topic of discussion and take up so much time and attention. Triggers can look like many things, but they lead to one of two places: depression or sin. Triggers that remind us of hurts from our past are seen as a very real threat to our way of life and freedom. We value our freedom, which is a God-given perspective, but that perspective can become skewed when we misidentify what freedom looks like. If we assume that freedom looks like control rather than self-control, we will set ourselves up in a way that makes ourselves our own source. In the same way that Adam and Eve chose to eat of the tree of the knowledge of good and evil, we can feel a sense of control but misidentify it as self-control and a fruit of the Spirit because our goal is to avoid sin. But, the end does not justify the means. Remember, control comes from a place of wanting to act as our own god and typically requires not only trying to control ourselves in our own strength, but also trying to control the people around us. Control and manipulation go hand-in-hand.

Self-control is a fruit of the Spirit and we access that fruit when we submit our control and desire for control to God. Adam and Eve reached for the fruit that gave them a sense of control over their lives. If they knew everything, including the bad, then they could avoid it. Which on the surface doesn't sounds so wrong, except that this isn't how God actually designed you to live. He designed you to live in connection to His Spirit that would cultivate in you the desires of His heart. And out of that connection, His desires would then become what you desire. You wouldn't need to be guided by your knowledge of right from wrong, because you would know God's heart. Living in this way, not only empowers you to live a life that conveys the heart of the Father, it also empowers you to do so in His power and not your own.

A common trigger for many people is the feeling of being misunderstood. Being misunderstood can feel awful. God has designed in us the need to be seen and known intimately. When we feel misunderstood, it can trigger a sense of loneliness. I have been there more times than I could count, and the pain of being misunderstood can hurt like few other things can. Feeling misunderstood is not only an attack on who we are but also an attack on our perception of control over our own lives. The trigger of misunderstanding and the belief that someone has more say over who we are than Jesus does, is a trap to hand over our own self-control to someone else. This trigger can send people into a spectrum of reactions anywhere from self-loathing and despair to a fit of rage and hate. That spectrum can lead us into either believing what that person has chosen to see us as, or it can lead us into a paradigm that tells us that we have to control what the other person who misunderstood us thinks so that they will believe what we want them to believe, or else we will punish them.  No matter where you are on that spectrum, it will ultimately lead you to a false sense of identity and into isolation and disconnection.

Many people have learned to recognize triggers. And I think that's a huge part of inner healing. But, it's what we do with that information that is going to determine whether or not we are going to live in true freedom or a synthesized version of freedom. The most common idea is to set

———

Whatever you order your life around has the preeminence in your life. Whatever you protect, *you assign value to*. Whatever you order your life around, you serve, even if it is ordered as a means to avoid it.

———

perimeters and safeguards in your life in order to avoid the triggers that you have identified. That can look like cutting off a relationship with someone you disagree with because you feel that if that subject that you disagree on comes up in conversation, it will trigger you into a response that you cannot control. It can look like organizing your life in order to avoid the feeling of rejection or failure in order to protect yourself from what you believe would be an inevitable downward spiral. The problem with all of these is what you have subtly believed about yourself. You thought you were dealing with propensities, but you were actually partnering with a lie that told you that who you are is determined by what has set you off before, and if presented with the same trigger again, you will fall into it again because you are a slave to that trigger. You have believed your identity has a flaw that is not redeemable, only manageable. You have believed a lie that you can be controlled by external forces rather than living in the freedom of the fruit of the Spirit known as self-control.

Whatever you order your life around has the preeminence in your life. Whatever you protect, you assign value to. Whatever you order your life around, you serve, even if it is ordered as a means to avoid it.

If we order our lives around avoiding the triggers we have believed to have such great power over us, then we have abandoned the idea of freedom in Jesus. Then we've chosen instead the idea that if we can harness our own power of avoiding those danger zones and carving out a path for ourselves that protects us from ever having to deal with the root that caused the triggers in the first place, then we will be free.

If you were to see your life as a road map, and you routed out your course by way of avoiding your triggers, then your life would be guided by your triggers rather than your God. If we follow the path of avoidance, we will submit to the idea that we are slaves to our triggers. We will keep our eyes on the danger zones to stay away from them. We will base our lives on the narrowness of our experiences rather than the greatness of our God.

I think Jesus summed this us brilliantly:

> Jesus replied (to the Pharisees), "You're right that you only
> have my word. But you can depend on it being true. I
> know where I've come from and where I go next. You

> don't know where I'm from or where I'm headed. You
> decide according to what you can see and touch. I don't
> make judgments like that. But even if I did, my judgment
> would be true because I wouldn't make it out of the
> narrowness of my experience but in the largeness of the
> One who sent me, the Father." John 8:14-16 (MSG)

Your origin is paramount. Who God designed and created you to be is your true identity. And He made you to be in His Presence, because you have been made alive in His Son. The battle is for your belief. If we assign power to our triggers, we will always be more impressed with what haunts us rather than the work that Jesus did to set us free. We are no longer slaves, so why would we bind ourselves to a life of servitude to our fears?

When I was walking through my season of post-partem depression, my fears controlled my every thought, feeling, and decision. The devil wants you to live in fear because fear is paralyzing. Fear causes you to turn inward and become trapped within your own mind. I tried to label what I was fearing in that time as a fear of germs or disease and sickness. But, truly what I feared was my children becoming sick by something I did. I was afraid of myself. I was afraid that if I didn't keep their environment completely sterile that I would have failed in my responsibility to care for them, and if that happened, I was sure that it meant that I didn't do my best for them. I feared that I would be selfish and choose laziness or apathy if I didn't consider every moment a potential threat to my children and therefore stand in battle stance against a potential pathogen at all times. I thought that if I let go of complete control and let myself think of anything or do anything other than constantly fighting an invisible war against germs, that I would have failed my children. So, my every waking moment and even the few moments of sleep that I would get in that time, were of constant worry and fear in an effort to always stay alert and to never make a mistake for my children. I was afraid I wasn't good enough .

The enemy always attacks with a lie about who God is and who you are. His goal is for you to fear yourself. Where can you go if you fear yourself? You are trapped. You hate yourself and yet simultaneously worship yourself. You find yourself unworthy of a good God while becoming your own god. Whatever your fear you worship. We can fear ourselves as our own deity

I was afraid of who I thought
I was, and that was what
led me to try to control
everything in my own
strength and brought me to
the end of myself. If I chose
to walk away from what fear
told me, it would have to
mean that *I would surrender
my control to God.*

and believe control is better than surrender to God, and assume the role of savior in our own lives. Or we can fear ourselves with self-hatred. Often times, the lies we believe about ourselves, are the things that we hate about ourselves. Just as Erika had believed, her greatest obstacle was her belief about her identity. The enemy is indifferent to how you fear yourself. His goal is for you to fear yourself because whatever you fear, you worship. You can worship yourself by believing you have no need of God, but you can also worship yourself by believing you are not loved by God. You can fear yourself to the point of suicide. This is the final act of being your own god and your self being the one your fear the most. The enemy's strategy is to make you the savior of your life, good or bad, because you are the one person you cannot escape from and ultimately it is what you believe about yourself and about God that will determine your choices.

I didn't understand this cycle of fear while I was living in that dark season of postpartum depression. For me to get to this place of testimony, it took being entirely vulnerable with the Lord so He could lead me through to healing and freedom. And in that process, God would continue to bring revelation, truth and healing. He was taking me from glory to glory. But, I had to bring, as a sacrifice to the Lord, every fear that I had held so tightly. I had to let go of whatever wisdom I thought I had gained from fear and control and stand in front of God with nothing less than everything and leave it all with Him. I didn't ignore the problem; I had to recognize there was a problem. I didn't just have one trigger. Everything around me triggered me. Every decision and movement I made was a trigger for me. I had to make a choice. Who would I serve? My fears? Myself? Or would I serve God in worship with a holy fear and reverence of Him? Would I acknowledge in my soul that He is God over my life and my children's lives? Would I believe His Word to be true over my crippling fears that felt so real? Doing so would bring me to a point where my ultimate trigger would have to be confronted.

When I had the intense urge to react to the fear of "what if," engaging with the invisible enemy of germs that demanded my attention, would I turn away from the lies and turn to God instead? This would have meant that the fear of not doing everything in my power to protect my kids from sickness would be triggered. Because this fear had such a grip on me, I had to make that choice all day every day. If I didn't rearrange my entire life even if just for a miniscule chance of not having a completely sterile environment, I would

We can position
ourselves for battle to
war against ourselves
and our inner thoughts
and feelings. *Or we can
look to the humanity
of Jesus.*

instantly feel like a terrible mother. I thought I was dealing with a crippling fear of my children becoming sick, but at its core, I was actually afraid of myself. I was afraid of who I thought I was, and that was what led me to try to control everything in my own strength and brought me to the end of myself. If I chose to walk away from what my fear told me, it would have to mean that I would surrender my control to God. Even what I thought I was surrendering to the Lord wasn't the entirety of what I needed to turn away from, but it was a start. I didn't only have to believe God's protection and health for my children, I had to believe Him about His identity and mine. In bringing all that I had to God, He gave me all that He has which is always a better exchange. I had no idea how much I had built my life at that time around a tangled web of lies that were keeping me distracted from what I was really ordering my life around. I had to exchange the fear I used as my guide, in all of its inferiority, for the original intent of righteous fear, which is reverence for the holiness of and goodness of God. True worship is our response to who God is and our surrender to Him.

Identifying triggers should lead us into the presence of God, not slavery. Identifying triggers shows us what we have to give to God, exchanging them for what He has for us.

True freedom is not found in carefully orchestrating our lives in the avoidance of triggers or in the meticulously controlled and barricaded life, but in the healing presence of God. Your life begins to speak His goodness when you see yourself as God sees you and you live in the freedom of the Truth. And this can only happen when we look up to see who Jesus is.

We can position ourselves for battle to war against ourselves and our inner thoughts and feelings. Or we can look to the humanity of Jesus. We take on the battle plan of starving our flesh over and over again. Or we can look to the battle that Jesus fought for us. We can look to our own hands and see weapons of war in our own strength, or we can look to the hands of Jesus and see the battle scars of a war already fought and won. The hands and feet of Jesus still show the scars of the nails that were driven into Him. These scars are not a memory of defeat. They are banners of victory. They are a symbol to find rest in the work of His hands, and peace in the path that He has walked ahead of us to secure.

True freedom is not found
in carefully orchestrating our
lives in the avoidance
of triggers or in the
meticulously controlled and
barricaded life, *but in the
healing presence of God.*

If we are fighting ourselves, then we have assumed ourselves to be the enemy. And therefore, we have assigned our identity to be at war with God. If God is holy and we are flesh, then we have taken on an identity that says who we really are is apart from God. And that is the same lie the serpent told Eve. The lie was always about her identity. The enemy told her she wasn't made in His image because she didn't have all that God has. The devil was banking on Eve not believing her true identity. It's this belief that brings us right back to the lie of separation between us and God when, for a believer, there is now no more separation. Jesus took our separation for us. Warring our flesh forms an identity of ourselves that has nothing to do with Jesus and everything to do with ourselves.

As Ephesians 6:12 tells us, we do not wrestle against flesh and blood. Not even our own.

A tree starts with a single seed. That is the tree's origin. The seed determines the tree. In other words, the seed determines the identity of the tree. When Adam and Eve had to leave the garden, the only seed they could take with them was the seed inside of Adam. In his seed, was the inherent separation of sin. Mankind was separated from God. Every person born from that time was born of a woman and the seed of man. Until Jesus.

"He was not born by the joining of human parents or from natural means, or by a man's desire, but he was born of God." John 1:13 TPT

"Gabriel answered (Mary), "The Spirit of Holiness will fall upon you and the almighty God will spread his shadow of power over you in a cloud of glory! This is why the child born to you will be holy, and he will be called the Son of God." Luke 1:35 TPT

Jesus was not born of the seed of man. Jesus was conceived by the power of the Holy Spirit. His Father was God. Jesus was fully God because He was conceived of the seed of the Spirit of God, and fully Man because He was carried and birthed by a woman.  This is how Jesus is fully God and fully Man. Sin and separation were not inherent to Jesus because He was of the Seed of God. His identity and inherent nature were as the Son of God.

"Keep in mind that we who belong to Jesus, the Anointed One, have already experienced crucifixion. For everything connected with our self-life was put to death on the cross and crucified with Messiah." Galatians 5:24 (TPT)

"My old identity has been co-crucified with Messiah and no longer lives; **for the nails of his cross crucified me with him**. And now the essence of this new life is no longer mine, for the Anointed One lives his life through me - **we live in union as one!**" Galatians 2:20 (TPT)

When you received salvation, Jesus breathed His Holy Spirit into you and made you alive in Him. You became born again. The death that Jesus died was the death of the seed of man, as He took your sin and separation upon Himself. The seed of Adam produced an identity that was apart from God even though you were made in the image of God. Your spirit was dead, and your flesh was alive. The greatest exchange ever made was your dead spirit and flesh for the resurrected life of Jesus. Your spirit awoke to His Presence and your flesh became obsolete. Where you were once a slave to separation and sin, you have been freed to see your true identity as a child of God.

Peter's vision in the book of Acts represented the heart of the Father for the gentiles: all are welcomed in His family. It gives us a clear picture of how God sees us. When Peter referred to the animals in the sheet representing what was considered unclean in the Jewish customs, God spoke this truth, "Nothing is unclean if God declares it to be clean." Acts 10:15( TPT)

What has the enemy told you about your identity? What have you been told to avoid and to live in fear of rather than being set free from the inside out? Where have you believed a lie about who you are and need to exchange that for the truth of your true identity? When God exchanges His Truth for the lies about you, He is giving you a new standard to measure every belief against. If what you have been ordering your life around tells you something in contradiction with the word that God gave you, then you can immediately see it as a lie. You have what God says about you to set as your standard and anything that does not match that standard is not true of you. The system of a life lived with triggers as your road map and sin as your inheritance, sets up a cyclical obstacle course that keeps you from living the life of freedom and influence to the world around you that you have been born to live. It keeps you stuck in the same place, but you have been called to move forward! If you aren't sure what God says about, then now is the time to start that conversation with Him. He's ready, because He's been speaking your true identity over you since He formed you in your mother's womb.

What has God declared about you? You have been made holy and spotless to stand in the Presence of God. Jesus has given you all that He is. He shares His identity with you. When you received Jesus, you became born again of the Seed of God. What is inherently true of Jesus is inherently true of you because you have been born again of the Seed of God and you have been redeemed by the blood of Jesus. You have been made the righteousness of God in Christ Jesus. You have been given the right to become children of God by the Spirit of adoption. The same Spirit of Holiness as the Spirit that conceived Jesus in Mary's womb and that raised Christ from the dead is the Spirit that has made you alive to your identity in Christ. You are of the Seed of God through and through. This adoption is not only legal, but it has transfused the blood of Jesus into your veins. You are a child of God by blood. By the blood of Jesus, you are legally and rightfully of the lineage of God.

The flesh that was inherent to sin is no longer alive in you. We have to see our flesh as the body of Jesus that was crucified. We cannot adhere to the belief that as a child of God, our sin is still alive. Jesus took our flesh upon Himself and that was how He sacrificed Himself for us. He died carrying our flesh. We have to appropriate the death of Jesus on the cross with the death of our flesh. The death of Jesus on the cross was the death of sin, separation, and the flesh that bore them. We can only acknowledge the resurrection of Christ if we first acknowledge the death of the Savior. And so it is with our flesh, we can only acknowledge our new nature in Christ if we first acknowledge the death of our flesh.

Jesus' words in John 8:34-36 (TPT) speak this, "When you sin you are not free. You've become a slave to sin. And slaves have no permanent standing in a family, like a son does, for a son is a part of the family forever. So, if the Son sets you free from sin, then become a true son and be unquestionably free!"

You are not a slave to triggers. The denial of triggers and the safeguarding of triggers is not the freedom Jesus died for you to have. When we look to Jesus, we can see what Jesus took for us, so we can give him every trigger in exchange for His freedom. We can let go of what we once believed to have power over us and pick up instead the words that the Father speaks over us. When God speaks to you who you are, that is your new standard. You never have to leave an encounter with God empty handed. He has a word for you that speaks to you who He is and who you are. It is in Spirit-to-spirit communion that we have a relationship with the Father so that we can live in the healing and freedom of Jesus as a child of God, just as Jesus is. What is inherent to you now is the nature of Christ.

Perhaps, the greatest struggle a Christian faces is the lie of the nature of sin. While the word triggers is most often referring to reminders of past trauma and the potential to wound someone again, that word is also used to describe propensities for sin. Much like triggers for hurt, triggers for sin are commonly believed to be a blueprint for how to avoid what we don't want to see in our lives and therefore we are careful to make the triggers as big as we can make them in our eyes in order to avoid them. The common belief is that we are at war within ourselves to not do the sin that we want to do. The phrase, dying to the flesh, is a very well-known phrase in Christian circles. But, so often that phrase has become lost in translation and many Christians believe is that their flesh is alive and well. And that their flesh is the most dominant part of them. They believe the flesh tells them who they really are - a sinner saved by grace. This communicates that there was not a transformation and an exchange of seed at the moment of salvation, only a change in our destination. Heaven instead of hell. Inside this paradigm is the belief that our identity is a sinner, and our lives on earth are a continual denial of who we really are until we get to heaven where we can finally be free.

The enemy wants to convince you that who you really are is a sinner and in an effort to solidify this lie in your mind, he will present you with what we call temptation. In our culture, temptation is recognized as anything that you want to do but should not do. We've been taught that temptation denotes a desire to do something wrong. The idea is that you are inherently prone to sin and your true nature wants to sin, but becoming a Christian means you need to pretend to not be who you really are and pretend to be like Jesus instead. The common theme is that your identity as a sinner hasn't changed, you have just chosen to try really hard not to sin.

So then, from now on, we have a new perspective that

———

As Ephesians 6:12 tells us, we do not wrestle against flesh and blood. *Not even our own.*

———

refuses to evaluate people merely by their outward
appearances. For that's how we once viewed the Anointed
One, but no longer do we see him with limited human
insight. Now, if anyone is enfolded into Christ, he has
become an entirely new person. All that is related to the
old order has vanished. Behold, everything is fresh and
new. And God has made all things new, and reconciled us
to himself, and given us the ministry of reconciling others
to God. 2 Corinthians 5:16-18 (TPT)

To say you are fighting or starving or putting to death your flesh sounds
so pious, but in reality, it's denying that Jesus took on your sin nature at
the cross and at your salvation, exchanged it for His righteous Son nature.
Inherent in Jesus is the sinless nature that has no desire to do wrong. When
Jesus breathed His Spirit in you, you became one with Him in Spirit. Your
nature changed. Your identity changed. Your desires, when realized, are
only to do what pleases God. You don't have a sinful bone in your body,
but you do have a free will. You have a mind that has the freedom to believe
whatever you choose.

There are three things you need in order to sin: to believe a lie about your
identity, believe a lie about the identity of God, and have free will. This does
not make you a sinner. It makes you a free being. His nature is not control;
His nature is love. And in Him is all freedom. With the Holy Spirit as your
Source of life, He will remind you of who you are when you are given the
temptation to sin. Any desire to sin does not come from who you are, but
from a lie about who you are and about who God is.

As a man believes in his heart, so is he. If you believe that you are inherently
prone to sin, your thoughts and your actions will follow. If the enemy can
convince you that you are a sinner saved by grace, then you will engage in a
battle that was fought long ago. That battle ended. The sin nature in you died.
To fight your flesh would mean to fight a dead and powerless foe that Jesus
defeated and wiped away from you. To deny your new nature is to deny the
exchange that Jesus made for you.

We know Jesus in that new way, Spirit to spirit, because we have been born
again in the Seed, Jesus, who has eradicated the sin nature and resurrected

us to have His blood in our veins and His nature in our spirits. We have the mind of Christ if we will just turn our hearts to His.

When the devil tempted Jesus in the wilderness, it didn't mean that Satan knew what Jesus' heart really wanted. Jesus didn't really want to jump off the cliff, or reign over the earthly kingdoms. Jesus knew His identity; He knew where He came from and where He was going. He saw Satan fall like lightning. He already was the Beginning and the End. He was the spotless lamb then too. He had the ability to sin, though. He was free to choose a lie and to sin, but there was no sin in His heart or evil desire in Him. Temptation doesn't illuminate your evil desires. Temptation is merely a suggestion from the enemy. Don't let the devil tell you who you are or what you want. Jesus didn't and neither should you. What we have been calling temptation, would in our current culture, be better described as opportunity. This speaks to not only the failure of the enemy and his loss of authority, but to your identity in Christ.

The devil wants to convince you, but he also wants you to try to convince him. He wants you to feel like you have to disprove the lies because he wants your attention. And he wants you to spend all that time in your head trying to prove him wrong, so that he can actually determine your thoughts. He wants your thoughts ordered around his lies, instead of what God is speaking. As Proverbs 23:7 teaches us - as a man believes in his heart, so is he, therefore so he behaves. Your behavior follows your heart. The battle is for your belief. The devil will lie about your identity, but he can't change your identity. He will, however, try to keep you focused on his lies and hold your attention, even if your goal in doing so is to prove him wrong.

Temptation doesn't really say anything about who you are, but it does tell you about the enemy's strategy. With each temptation, the enemy is risking being found out. With each offer to sin, the enemy is daring to come close to a child of God who carries the Spirit of the Risen Lamb and who looks just like Jesus.

> So now the case is closed. There remains no accusing
> voice of condemnation against those who are joined in
> life-union with Jesus, the Anointed One. For the "law" of
> the Spirit of life flowing through the anointing of Jesus

has liberated us from the "law" of sin and death. For God achieved what the law was unable to accomplish, because the law was limited by the weakness of human nature. Yet God sent us his Son in human form to identify with human weakness. Clothed with humanity, God's Son gave his body to be the sin-offering so that God could once and for all condemn the guilt and power of sin. So now every righteous requirement of the law can be fulfilled through the Anointed One living his life in us. And we are free to live, not according to our flesh, but by the dynamic power of the Holy Spirit! Those who are motivated by the flesh only pursue what benefits themselves. But those who live by the impulses of the Holy Spirit are motivated to pursue spiritual realities. For the mind-set of the flesh is death, but the mind-set controlled by the Spirit finds life and peace. In fact, the mind-set focused on the flesh fights God's plan and refuses to submit to his direction, because it cannot! For no matter how hard they try, God finds no pleasure with those who are controlled by the flesh. But when the Spirit of Christ empowers your life, you are not dominated by the flesh but by the Spirit. And if you are not joined to the Spirit of the Anointed One, you are not of him. Now Christ lives his life in you! And even though your body may be dead because of the effects of sin, his life-giving Spirit imparts life to you because you are fully accepted by God. Yes, God raised Jesus to life! And since God's Spirit of Resurrection lives in you, he will also raise your dying body to life by the same Spirit that breathes life into you! So then, beloved ones, the flesh has no claims on us at all, and we have no further obligation to live in obedience to it. For when you live controlled by the flesh, you are about to die. But if the life of the Spirit puts to death the corrupt ways of the flesh, we then taste his abundant life. Romans 8:1-13 (TPT)

We have to learn that there is a defined distinction between flesh and humanity because of Seed! The flesh of the sin nature and our humanity

Jesus, being fully God and fully Man, is not a walking contradiction. Instead, Jesus is *our perfect example of what God created humanity to become.* He is the exact image of your *true nature when you became a child of God.*

adopted by the Spirit of God are two different things. One lives in enmity with God. The other is the expression of heaven on earth, of God and man in partnership the way we were created to be, in order to see His will on this earth as it is in heaven.

Jesus, being fully God and fully Man, is not a walking contradiction. Instead, Jesus is our perfect example of what God created humanity to become. He is the exact image of your true nature when you became a child of God. The First of Many is the One who showed us what humanity was always intended to be. Flesh and free will are not synonymous. Sin is an option you are free to choose, but it goes against every fiber of your being. Jesus was not hindered as a man by a sin nature or flesh, but instead was empowered by the nature of God that partnered with His humanity to see heaven on earth. When you have been raised to a new life in Jesus, you do not become a sinner, saved by grace. You become a child of God with the nature of Jesus to live on this earth as He did. This is the beauty of Jesus being fully God and fully man. Humanity was designed to live in Him.

This is not about convincing yourself that you are good. This is about seeing Jesus for who He is. Sin is within your capability. And your responsibility to walk in obedience to God is not negated because of your new nature in Christ. On the contrary, you have been left with no excuse to sin. It's not who you are. And when you live your life viewing a sin nature as your greatest obstacle, then you have minimized in your eyes the sinless life Jesus lived to give you. When you order your life around not sinning, you have neglected the resurrection life that is in you. When you hold to the belief that your sin nature is alive and well, you have abandoned the righteousness of Jesus and His blood that had made you alive, defeating death and sin. When you live with the belief that you are at war with a sin nature, you are neglecting the truth that Jesus lives in you. You have put yourself as a building with two different foundations. And a house divided cannot stand,

When you order your life around avoiding sin, you have made sin your route-marker and guide.

When you live with the belief that you are inherent by identity to sin, you are living in neglect of the truth of your identity in Christ. He didn't come to give you an idea of being sinless because you're forgiven yet not transformed. You have been made new and redeemed and through the identity of Christ and the Seed of God you are not only sinless, but you have died forever to the seed of man that made sin inherent to the identity of sin. The nature of sin and the nature of God cannot coexist inside of you. The free will to sin is always available to you, even if you're not inherent to sin anymore. But the belief of a false identity will cause you to behave in the way you believe about yourself.

The biggest obstacle to a believer is not a dead and powerless sin nature. The biggest obstacle is the belief that you are inherently a sinner. Though triggers and temptations can be good indicators of where you need soul healing, they do not give you your identity.

The belief that you are inherent to sin is in direct opposition to the truth that you have been made alive as a Child of God, a joint heir with Christ, and that you share His divine nature. You have been raised to a new life with Christ and now born again of the Seed of God and inherent to you is now the nature of Christ.

> Everything we could ever need for life and godliness has already been deposited in us by his divine power. For all this was lavished upon us through the rich experience of knowing him who has called us by name and invited us to come to him through a glorious manifestation of his goodness. As a result of this, he has given you magnificent promises that are beyond all price, so that through the power of these tremendous promises you can experience partnership with the divine nature, by which you have escaped the corrupt desires that are of the world. 2 Peter 1:3-4 (TPT)

With this fresh perspective, I want you to grab your Bible and read Romans 7 and 8 with Jesus. These chapters have been shouting the truth of your new nature for thousands of years.

> For we know that the law is divinely inspired and comes from the spiritual realm, but I am a human being made of flesh and trafficked as a slave under sin's authority. I'm a mystery to myself, for I want to do what is right, but end

up doing what my moral instincts condemn. And if my behavior is not in line with my desire, my conscience still confirms the excellence of the law. And now I realize that it is no longer my true self doing it, but the unwelcome intruder of sin in my humanity. For I know that nothing good lives within the flesh of my fallen humanity. The longings to do what is right are within me, but willpower is not enough to accomplish it. My lofty desires to do what is good are dashed when I do the things I want to avoid. So, if my behavior contradicts my desires to do good, I must conclude that it's not my true identity doing it, but the unwelcome intruder of sin hindering me from being who I really am. Through my experience of this principle, I discover that even when I want to do good, evil is ready to sabotage me. Truly, deep within my true identity, I love to do what pleases God. But I discern another power operating in my humanity, waging a war against the moral principles of my conscience and bringing me into captivity as a prisoner to the "law" of sin—this unwelcome intruder in my humanity. What an agonizing situation I am in! So, who has the power to rescue this miserable man from the unwelcome intruder of sin and death? I give all my thanks to God, for his mighty power has finally provided a way out through our Lord Jesus, the Anointed One! So, if left to myself, the flesh is aligned with the law of sin, but now my renewed mind is fixed on and submitted to God's righteous principles. Romans 7:1-25 (TPT)

The difference is Jesus. His death on the cross became your death. What was once true about humanity apart from God is no longer true when your humanity is met with the divine nature of God and the Seed of Jesus. We were never designed to want to sin, but a life apart from Jesus awakens those desires to sin. When we recognize who God always intended us to be, we find that Jesus is our only Savior. He is our Redeemer, bringing us back to our origin. There is freedom in Jesus not only to live our lives well on the outside, but to also be free from the triggers and desires that want to tear us down on the inside. He is inviting you to know freedom in Him in a new way. This is the heart of God for all humanity - for us to live Spirit to spirit.

Romans 8:1-39 perfectly explains everything we've discussed in this chapter. I have found in my own life that there are verses in the Bible that I had read so many times but had never realized how much those words communicated. This is a long section of the Bible but I decided to put the full chapter in this book because I want to encourage you to let Jesus speak these verses to you on your own journey with Him. My hope is that these verses will be illuminated in a new and revelatory way as you read these words with Him.

> So now the case is closed. There remains no accusing voice of condemnation against those who are joined in life-union with Jesus, the Anointed One. For the "law" of the Spirit of life flowing through the anointing of Jesus has liberated us from the "law" of sin and death. For God achieved what the law was unable to accomplish, because the law was limited by the weakness of human nature. Yet God sent us his Son in human form to identify with human weakness. Clothed with humanity, God's Son gave his body to be the sin-offering so that God could once and for all condemn the guilt and power of sin. So now every righteous requirement of the law can be fulfilled through the Anointed One living his life in us. And we are free to live, not according to our flesh, but by the dynamic power of the Holy Spirit! Those who are motivated by the flesh only pursue what benefits themselves. But those who live by the impulses of the Holy Spirit are motivated to pursue spiritual realities. For the mind-set of the flesh is death, but the mind-set controlled by the Spirit finds life and peace. In fact, the mind-set focused on the flesh fights God's plan and refuses to submit to his direction, because it cannot! For no matter how hard they try, God finds no pleasure with those who are controlled by the flesh. But when the Spirit of Christ empowers your life, you are not dominated by the flesh but by the Spirit. And if you are not joined to the Spirit of the Anointed One, you are not of him. Now Christ lives his life in you! And even though your body may be dead because of the effects of sin, his life-giving Spirit imparts life to you because you are fully

accepted by God. Yes, God raised Jesus to life! And since God's Spirit of Resurrection lives in you, he will also raise your dying body to life by the same Spirit that breathes life into you! So then, beloved ones, the flesh has no claims on us at all, and we have no further obligation to live in obedience to it. For when you live controlled by the flesh, you are about to die. But if the life of the Spirit puts to death the corrupt ways of the flesh, we then taste his abundant life. The mature children of God are those who are moved by the impulses of the Holy Spirit. And you did not receive the "spirit of religious duty," leading you back into the fear of never being good enough. But you have received the "Spirit of full acceptance," enfolding you into the family of God. And you will never feel orphaned, for as he rises up within us, our spirits join him in saying the words of tender affection, "Beloved Father!" For the Holy Spirit makes God's fatherhood real to us as he whispers into our innermost being, "You are God's beloved child!" And since we are his true children, we qualify to share all his treasures, for indeed, we are heirs of God himself. And since we are joined to Christ, we also inherit all that he is and all that he has. We will experience being co-glorified with him provided that we accept his sufferings as our own. I am convinced that any suffering we endure is less than nothing compared to the magnitude of glory that is about to be unveiled within us. The entire universe is standing on tiptoe, yearning to see the unveiling of God's glorious sons and daughters! For against its will the universe itself has had to endure the empty futility resulting from the consequences of human sin. But now, with eager expectation, all creation longs for freedom from its slavery to decay and to experience with us the wonderful freedom coming to God's children. To this day we are aware of the universal agony and groaning of creation, as if it were in the contractions of labor for childbirth. And it's not just creation. We who have already experienced the first fruits of the Spirit also inwardly groan as we passionately long to experience our full status as

God's sons and daughters–including our physical bodies being transformed. For this is the hope of our salvation. But hope means that we must trust and wait for what is still unseen. For why would we need to hope for something we already have? So because our hope is set on what is yet to be seen, we patiently keep on waiting for its fulfillment. And in a similar way, the Holy Spirit takes hold of us in our human frailty to empower us in our weakness. For example, at times we don't even know how to pray, or know the best things to ask for. But the Holy Spirit rises up within us to super-intercede on our behalf, pleading to God with emotional sighs too deep for words. God, the searcher of the heart, knows fully our longings, yet he also understands the desires of the Spirit, because the Holy Spirit passionately pleads before God for us, his holy ones, in perfect harmony with God's plan and our destiny. So we are convinced that every detail of our lives is continually woven together to fit into God's perfect plan of bringing good into our lives, for we are his lovers who have been called to fulfill his designed purpose. For he knew all about us before we were born and he destined us from the beginning to share the likeness of his Son. This means the Son is the oldest among a vast family of brothers and sisters who will become just like him. Having determined our destiny ahead of time, he called us to himself and transferred his perfect righteousness to everyone he called. And those who possess his perfect righteousness he co-glorified with his Son! So, what does all this mean? If God has determined to stand with us, tell me, who then could ever stand against us? For God has proved his love by giving us his greatest treasure, the gift of his Son. And since God freely offered him up as the sacrifice for us all, he certainly won't withhold from us anything else he has to give. Who then would dare to accuse those whom God has chosen in love to be his? God himself is the judge who has issued his final verdict over them– "Not guilty!" Who then is left to condemn us? Certainly not Jesus, the Anointed One! For he gave his life for us, and even more than that, he has conquered death and is now risen, exalted, and enthroned by God at his right hand. So how could he possibly condemn us since he is continually praying for our triumph? Who could ever separate us from the endless love of God's Anointed One? Absolutely no one! For nothing in the universe has the power to diminish his love toward us. Troubles, pressures, and problems are unable to come between us and heaven's love. What about persecutions, deprivations, dangers, and death threats? No, for they are all impotent to hinder omnipotent love, even though it is written: All day long we face death threats for your sake, God. We are considered to be nothing more than sheep to be slaughtered! Yet even in the midst of all these things, we triumph over them all, for God has made us to be more than conquerors, and his demonstrated love is our glorious victory over everything! So now I live with the confidence that there is nothing in the universe with the power to separate us from God's love. I'm convinced that his love will triumph over death, life's troubles, fallen angels, or dark rulers in the heavens. There is nothing in our present or future circumstances that can weaken his love. There is no power above us or beneath us—no power that could ever be found in the universe that can distance us from God's passionate love, which is lavished upon us through our Lord Jesus, the Anointed One! (TPT)

To say that you are bound to triggers or bound by sin is to deny the humanity of Jesus. Jesus laid down His deity to take on our humanity. Being fully God, not born by the seed of man, but also fully human having come from the Seed of God, He was the First to live Spirit to spirit and heaven to earth.

"He didn't need anyone to tell him about human nature, for he fully understood what man was capable of doing." John 2:25 (TPT)

Jesus understood because everything that is needed to sin was true about Him, too. He lived in our humanity and yet was without sin. And the same power has been made available to us as part of our inheritance here and now. His humanity did not hold Him back or hinder the anointing or call the Father gave Him. And neither will it hinder you if you walk in the truth of the identity of Christ. He laid down His deity to make the way for us to fully realize our humanity in Him. To believe you are a slave to sin and flesh denies the crushing He took for us so that He could break the chains of slavery and sin on us. To deny your new nature as a child of God is to deny the sacrifice He made for you to become like Him. If the Son has set you free, you are free indeed.

The choice Jesus made to come to earth as Man  was not for a temporary time on earth. This decision was forever. Jesus is raised to Life and seated at the right hand of the Father as the Son of God, who is fully God and Fully Man, so that we can be seated next to Him. Jesus lives this love for us and will throughout eternity. The sacrifice He made to become like us, so that we could become like Him, is a never-ending love song that He will sing over us for eternity. It is who He is.

"*By living in God*, love has been brought to its full expression in us so that we may fearlessly face the day of judgment, because all that Jesus now is, so are we in this world." 1 John 4:17 (TPT)

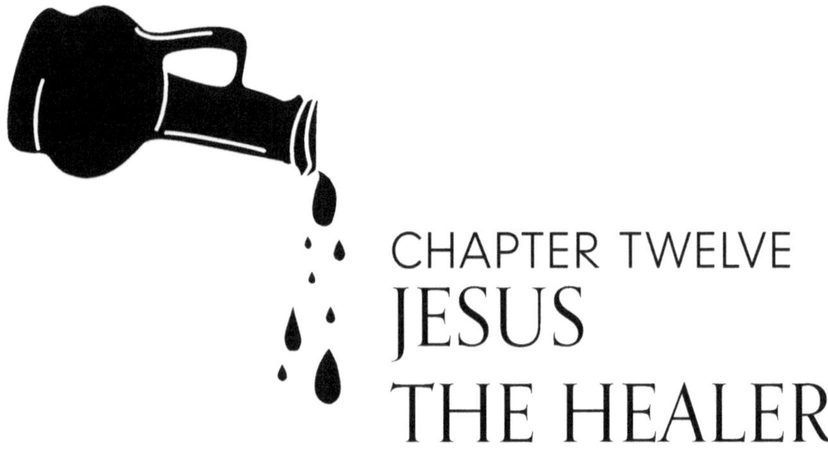

# CHAPTER TWELVE
# JESUS THE HEALER

Physical healing is a very diverse and somewhat elusive conversation in the modern church. There are many theologies surrounding this topic and even more lived experiences that would lead people to their own beliefs about healing. As I have quoted before in this book of the words of Jesus from John 8, we cannot base our theology on the narrowness of our experiences, but rather the greatness of our God. If Jesus is our example and the perfect image of the Father, then we must conclude that Jesus and the life He lived should be the standard for all Biblical theology. In accordance with every account written of Jesus, all who came to Him for healing were healed. It was not the magnitude of the sickness, injury, or even death that had the final say in each interaction with Jesus. It was Jesus, who focused on the greatness of His Father and did only what He saw the Father do, who had the final say. When Jesus was asked if He was willing to heal, the answer was yes. At no point did Jesus ever communicate a reality in which sometimes healing would not be done for them. This can be a painful truth for us to hear in our current time because so many Christians have lived experiences that would tell them otherwise. But, if we let ourselves make judgments based off of our own experiences, we start to mold the idea of who God is based off of our own understanding. We have to look to Jesus as our standard. There is a humility that comes from acknowledging that not everything in our world has happened according to the heart of the Father, but that it is possible to see heaven on earth and God's will to be done because of Jesus. Everything about Jesus tells us what is true about us. Who He is and all that He has is true of every believer who has become of the lineage of Christ. Jesus healed all who came to Him. And He told us to go and do the same that He did, and even greater. Healing is true of your identity because it is true of the identity of Jesus.

The numerous accounts of healings performed by Jesus recorded in the Gospels are merely a glimpse of how many Jesus performed. As John writes, all the books in the world could not contain all the miracles Jesus performed. Interestingly, we never read of Jesus Himself needing healing, prior to His sacrifice. He was always in full agreement with who God says He is. He always functioned out of HIs identity and the identity of His Father. Sickness and disease had no right or authority in His body because He was of the Seed of God. And as a child of God, the same is true of you. When Jesus was healing people, He was giving them what was true in Him. He was giving of Himself and sharing it with them.

Jesus gave healing because healing was true in His identity and because He lived in full agreement with His identity, He lived heaven on earth. What is true of Jesus, even His physical body, is true of you too. It's inherent to your bloodline and identity. The health of Jesus is your health. Our bodies will respond to our hearts. And our hearts will respond to our spirits. Conversely, our bodies and minds will also respond to other influences. The factor that determines which influences impact us is what we have set our hearts to believe. What are we allowing to influence our hearts? Are we living from the inside out - our spirit that is joined with the Spirit of God? Or are we functioning from the outside in - the inferior reality of earth and the lies from the enemy?

As previously noted, as a man believes in his heart, so is he. What have we been believing to be true of our bodies that is incongruent with our nature as a child of God? What have we accepted as inevitable when our true identities speak otherwise?

I know that everything about Jesus seems so idyllic. It seems as if He lived with an advantage that the rest of us don't have. But, the truth is that Jesus

———

Healing is true
of your identity because
*it is true of the identity*
*of Jesus.*

———

laid down His deity to take on our humanity. He lived from heaven to earth because He lived in the nature and bloodline that He has made true about you now. So, if you consider Jesus to have lived with a little extra help because His assignment was so crucial, then you will have to consider yourself at that same advantage. Because, Jesus in you means that "as He is, so are we in this world." 1 John 4:17 (AMP). Jesus lived in everything that was true of a Child of God. The health of heaven was in His body because He lived as a human partnered with the Spirit of God on earth. And that is your life, too. He laid down any advantage that He could have had so that He could fully take your place to save you.

God spoke something to my heart a few years ago that expressed an entirely new concept of His love for us. God spoke a command to me:

Be as passionate about your healing as Jesus is.

> But the time was close for the Jewish Passover to begin,
> so Jesus walked to Jerusalem. As he went into the temple
> courtyard, he noticed it was filled with merchants selling
> oxen, lambs, and doves for exorbitant prices, while others
> were overcharging as they exchanged currency behind
> their counters. So, Jesus found some rope and made it
> into a whip. Then he drove out every one of them and
> their animals from the courtyard of the temple, and he
> kicked over their tables filled with money, scattering it
> everywhere! And he shouted at the merchants, 'Get these
> things out of here! Don't you dare make my Father's house
> into a center for merchandise!' That's when his disciples
> remembered the Scripture: "I am consumed with a fiery
> passion to keep your house pure!" John 2:13-17 (TPT)

God brought me this account of what most people typically like to use as their excuse to get angry. I'm not so sure that validating a temper is the writer's greatest intention for this story. And I also do not believe that Jesus was acting out of rage, but rather passion.

As soon as the religious leaders saw what they mistakenly perceived to be bullying, they immediately questioned Jesus' authority.

> But the Jewish religious leaders challenged Jesus, "What
> authorization do you have to do this sort of thing? If God
> gave you this kind of authority, what supernatural sign
> will you show us to prove it" Jesus answered, "After you've
> destroyed this temple, I will raise it up again in three days."
> Then the Jewish leaders sneered, "This temple took forty-six
> years to build, and you mean to tell us that you will raise
> it up in three days?" But they didn't understand that Jesus
> was speaking of the "temple" of his body. But the disciples
> remembered his prophecy after Jesus rose from the dead,
> and believed both the Scripture and what Jesus had said.
> John 2:18-22 (TPT)

I picture the temple courtyard where Jesus drove out what didn't belong there. It wasn't the innermost part of the temple where God would allow His presence; it was an extension of that holy place. The courtyard, I believe, is meant to be symbolic of our bodies. Our bodies can be an extension of our innermost being where the Presence of God has made us alive in His Spirit. But a courtyard can also be influenced by outside influences that do not belong there. What we believe and know to be true of Jesus and therefore ourselves matters greatly. This is why the battle is for your belief.

The battle isn't really for your healing. By Jesus' stripes, you were healed. Healing is true of who you are. The battle is for your belief. Healing is not far off in heaven. Heaven is in you. Jesus is in you. Jesus didn't take those stripes on His back to hold your healing away from you. He didn't take on the sin that made sickness and disease inherent in your body apart from Him so that He could keep your healing from you.

When Jesus formed that whip out of rope, He was laser focused on defending and protecting His bride. He rose up against the sickness and disease that has ravaged the body of His beloved. It was because of His intense passion for the temple-your body-that He drove out what didn't belong. Jesus just wouldn't allow it. He would not allow it to have a right to be there. He would strip sickness and disease of its authority to destroy our bodies.

At the moment of your salvation, Jesus breathed His Spirit into you. You are the temple of the Holy Spirit. You house His Presence. You have been

———

Be as passionate
*about your healing
as Jesus is.*

———

made holy and clean. Your body has been given the inheritance to carry the Presence of God and bring heaven to earth.

Be as passionate about your healing as Jesus is. When Jesus saw the money exchanging and unjust selling of merchandise, He saw what does not belong in your body and He would not allow it. The passion that Jesus displayed for our healing has welled up in me. When I see people suffering in their bodies, I have this intense passion to drive out what does not belong. It's true of who Jesus is, and it's true of us too. We need to allow God to cultivate in us the passion and zeal to Jesus has for our healing. But this can only come when we first see it in Jesus.

Most of us know the scripture of 1 Peter 2:24 that tells us, by Jesus' stripes, we were healed. Those stripes were those of a whip, a whip that ripped the flesh of Jesus right off of His body for you. It's no coincidence that it's by those stripes of a whip that we are healed. When Jesus fashioned that whip and drove out what didn't belong in the temple courtyard, He was prophesying of your healing made true in you by the stripes that He would take on His back. Jesus was painting a picture of the passion He has for your healing. He was showing you how to do as He did because as He is, so are you in this world. He has given you authority over what does not belong in your body. And with the same passion and authority that He drove out what did not belong in the temple, so are you to drive out what does not belong in the temple of the Holy Spirit which is now your body. By His stripes you were healed, and you carry that healing, paid for by His stripes, just as He carried that whip.

Seeing what Jesus took in His body for us, we see His passion for our healing. He exchanged His humanity connected to God's Spirit, for our humanity connected to sin and death. To see His sacrifice is to see your life. To see His stripes is to see your healing.

What is God speaking over your body? What is the standard He has set for you to measure every word against? I was praying over a woman once, a Christian, who told me she was having very serious back pain. I asked the Holy Spirit what He was speaking over her, and He told me to speak over this woman that her "back was not deteriorating." In all honesty, I thought to myself, that kind of sounds like a weird thing to say. I didn't feel like the word "deteriorating" made much sense, but I spoke it anyway. When I finished praying over her, she looked at me and said, "Thank you so much for asking the Holy Spirit what He says about my back! My doctor literally just told me that my back was 'deteriorating,' but that's not what God says!" God spoke to us what was already true of her body and inherent to her identity. All she had to do was see herself the way God sees her. Jesus won the battle for her belief too.

When Jesus drove out what didn't belong in the temple courtyard that day, He wasn't being a bully. It was His Father's house. It belonged to Him, too. Jesus was living in His full authority and power as His Father's heir. Power expressed without authority is being a bully. But Jesus had all authority as the Son of God. Jesus lived as fully God and fully Man and this is what gave Him the authority and power to heal so that it would be on earth as it is in heaven. And you are a joint heir with Christ.

"But those who embraced him and took hold of his name were given authority to become the children of God!" John 1:12 (TPT)

As a child of God, you have the same authority as Jesus because He has seated you next to Him as joint heir. You have been made alive in His Spirit, and born into the power of the Holy Spirit. It is His presence in you. And His presence will flow to your body and even from you to others. That is how Jesus lived. Giving of what was true of Himself to us. Jesus, who created time, was not bound by time. He healed everyone who came to Him by the stripes He took, even before He took them. Jesus stood in His identity.

You are His mirror image. You can look to Jesus, and you can speak to what doesn't belong and drive it out. Hold up the truth of the stripes He took for your health. You can do what Jesus did. Be as passionate about your healing as Jesus is. You can take that stand because Jesus Himself stands beside you, and you can drive out what doesn't belong.

Paul was well aware of this truth. When a venomous snake jumped out of a fire and bit him, he didn't even pray! I think most of us, just seeing a snake leap out of a fire would have dropped to our knees in desperate prayer. But Paul had this snake's fangs driven into his flesh and he just ripped it off of his arm and went about his day. Paul lived so acutely aware of the identity of Jesus and the finished work of the cross, that he didn't see venom as a threat

———

To see His sacrifice is to
see your life. To see
*His stripes is*
*to see your healing.*

———

to his body. He saw the health of the resurrected body of Jesus as his own. The revelation of His identity was the voice of God resonating in his body. Your existence, and your body, are held by the voice of God. And His voice resonates in your body what He speaks over you. What is God speaking over you?

My friend Lindsay, whom I mentioned earlier in this book, much like Paul, lives a life that exemplifies this truth. The revelation of who Jesus is and the righteousness that He shares with her (and you) is a hallmark of her life.

Lindsay had been told by her doctor that he had found a uterine growth via ultrasound. He had been suspicious for a long time from other ultrasounds and, over time, the growth that had become very prominent. Lindsay had been trying to get pregnant for years. She was already the momma of a beautiful little girl named Holiday, and she and her husband David knew that God had put it on their hearts to have more children. But, Lindsay had been unable to conceive after her first child, and that's when the doctors started looking for answers. Once the uterine growth had been detected, the plan to remove it began with the very likely possibility of having to remove her uterus. None of this was God's will for her life, but removing her uterus didn't just mean disease, it would mean Lindsay would never be able to conceive again.

As Lindsay recounts the day her doctor told her he had found the growth, the overriding anthem in her heart was, "No! This growth is not allowed to be in my body!" Lindsay knew the truth. She knew her identity. The voice of God was resonating in her spirit and speaking to her the truth of who she is and all that she has. Out of her spirit flowed the truth that was alive in her spirit, and she opened her heart to let that truth come in and wash over her. What was washing over her was the truth that, as Jesus is in this world, so are we. These are the very words she spoke to me as she was recounting this story. She wasn't impressed with the size of the problem, because she was more impressed by the greatness of her God. As she was driving in her car after that ultrasound, she spoke to the growth, and she told it that it had to leave. She told the growth it had to go.

According to the plan that Lindsay's doctor had advised, she showed up for a follow up ultrasound in order for the doctor to determine the best course of action to remove the growth. But, in Lindsay's heart, this was already a done deal. As the technician performed the ultrasound to get a better look at the growth the doctor had found, she couldn't find anything. The doctor was in the room as the technician tried every angle to find what the doctor had seen, but Lindsay's uterus was in perfect health. As the doctor could see for himself that there was no longer a growth on her uterus, bewildered, he said, "All I can say is, what was there before, isn't there now!"

When God revealed to me the passion that Jesus has for our healing, He also revealed to me a new concept that I had never considered before. He told me that I am to speak to what doesn't belong and tell it to go. Jesus, driving out with a whip what didn't belong in the temple, was showing us how to hold up the stripes that He bore on His back from a whip. He was modeling how to use His authority that He has given us to drive out what doesn't belong in the temple of the Holy Spirit. You are the temple of the Holy Spirit. This is appropriating the victory of Jesus that He has made ours. This is us looking like Jesus. We are to speak to the sickness and disease, declaring the truth that by the stripes of Jesus we were healed, and then tell it to leave. Jesus would not allow it to be there, and just as He drove it out, so do we. Lindsay would only speak what God was speaking over her. She spoke to what didn't belong and she drove it out. She knew what was true about her because she knew what was true about Jesus. She identified with Jesus. As of this writing, a few years have gone by since that last ultrasound looking for the uterine growth. But, Lindsay has had a few ultrasounds since and for the best of reasons. Holiday is now a big sister to a beautiful little baby girl named Mabel that Lindsay gave birth to just a few months ago!

As God had been leading me through the revelation of healing from the story of Jesus and the temple, He sent another layer of revelation that has completely changed what I believed about healing. It was as if all of the sudden, the eyes of my heart were opened to this profound realization.

*Jesus never asked God to heal anyone.*

What? This sounds a little wrong, Or maybe a lot wrong.

But as I continued to dwell on what God was speaking to me, I started seeing that not only did Jesus never ask God to heal anyone, but Jesus' disciples, once they became alive in that upper room by the breath of the resurrected

Jesus, also never asked God to heal anyone.

Every time Jesus encountered sickness, disease, and death, He always spoke directly to it. He spoke to what didn't belong and drove it out. He commanded life and health into their bodies in place of what He drove out. He was giving them what was true in His body and making it true in theirs. He had been given the power and authority because of His identity. And Jesus not only knew this, but He also knew the heart of the Father. Jesus knew that God was not withholding healing. Jesus knew there was no vault in heaven locked down and only accessed by a rarely solved combination lock. Jesus had the heart of the Father, and His heart was to see heaven on earth. Jesus is passionate about our healing. And He proved it by the stripes He took for you.

When our oldest daughter, Ava, was 3 years old, we found out that she had a UTI. She had been in so much pain and we had spent hours at the urgent care just to try to get a sample. Ava was so scared, and the pain had been so intense. The doctor gave us an antibiotic for her, and we started her on it right away, but they had told us that it would take about a day before any of the pain would be relieved. I gave her juice all day to get her to urinate so that she could start moving out the infection. Even after countless cups of juice, she refused to use the bathroom because she just couldn't take how painful it was. It had been 14 hours and juice after juice, and still she refused to urinate. By that point, I was feeling so desperate. It was heartbreaking to see her  so afraid and in pain. We were upstairs in her playroom, and I continued to encourage her to go to the bathroom.

I basically pleaded for about an hour that night as she repeatedly refused. I was telling her over and over again how it would be ok. I didn't want to lie and say it wouldn't hurt, but I also wanted to convince her to go! By this point, she was so exhausted and so completely afraid. She kept her resolve to avoid the bathroom as she cried and cried out of fear of the inevitable pain. It was breaking my heart. As I watched her sit there in her playroom and feeling so desperate to see her tears, all of the sudden, she stopped crying. She paused and looked up at me and said so calmly, "Ok. I can go potty now. I know it won't hurt." And she stood up, walked to the bathroom and she finally went, and it was absolutely pain free! As I watched all of this happen right in front of me, I knew there was only one explanation. I looked at Ava with tears in my eyes after hours of trying to convince her, even though I knew it wasn't enough time for the medicine to have freed her from the pain, and I asked her, "Ava, who told you that it wouldn't hurt?" And she just looked at me and said in her sweet little voice, "God told me!"

When God spoke that to her heart, she immediately knew it was true. And His word was enough for her. This is how God speaks to you. What is God speaking over your body? What is He saying that is true about you because it is true of Jesus? Healing is inherent in who you are. Jesus not only carried healing, He Himself is divine health. And that divine health is yours, because as Jesus is in this world, so are you.

"He himself carried our sins in his body on the cross so that we would be dead to sin and live for righteousness. Our instant healing flowed from his wounding." 1 Peter 2:24 (TPT)

The seed of man that carried sin and all that was inherent to sin has died on the cross with Jesus, and you have been resurrected to your new identity and born again of the Seed of God. Inherent to your new identity is the life of the resurrected Savior and the health and healing of His body that He has made to be yours.

This healing is true of who you are, and it's also true of what Jesus has given to you to give to the people around you. Jesus did not keep what He had to Himself. Jesus said in Matthew 10:8 (NKJV), "freely you have received, freely give." Paul, being so aware of His identity, knew healing was his so deeply that even when a venomous snake jumped out of a fire and bit him, he just pulled off the snake and walked away.

"God kept releasing a flow of extraordinary miracles through the hands of Paul. Because of this, people took Paul's handkerchiefs and articles of clothing, even pieces of cloth that had touched his skin, laying them on the bodies of the sick, and diseases and demons left them and they were healed." Acts 19:11-12 (TPT)

Paul's intimate communion with Jesus kept him attuned to everything that was true about him. And because Paul believed this to be true of his identity, he also knew it was his to freely give to others. And this was not specific only to Paul. Paul had no greater advantage to knowing Jesus intimately than you do. Paul never knew Jesus on earth except by His Spirit. The same is true for you. His intimacy with Jesus was not because of anything he did, but it had everything to do with what Jesus did. He did the same for you. And the intimacy in which Paul knew Jesus, is yours as well.

Peter lived in the same way. There's a remarkable difference between Peter as a disciple and Peter as a born-again believer filled with the Spirit of God. Peter went from being told by Jesus that he sounded just like Satan and denying Jesus three times, to boldly bringing heaven to earth just like His Redeemer.

When the crippled beggar at The Gate Beautiful asked Peter for money, Peter gave us an example that I pray will resonate in your hearts as long as you are on this earth.

"So, when he saw Peter and John about to go into the temple, he began asking [them] for coins. But Peter, along with John, stared at him intently and said, "Look at us!" And the man began to pay attention to them, eagerly expecting to receive something from them. But Peter said, "Silver and gold I do not have; but what I do have I give to you: In the name (authority, power) of Jesus Christ the Nazarene– [begin now to] walk and go on walking!" Then he seized the man's right hand with a firm grip and raised him up. And at once his feet and ankles became strong and steady, and with a leap he stood up and began to walk; and he went into the temple with them, walking and leaping and praising God." Acts 3:3-8 (AMP)

*What I do have, I give you.*

That grips me. Peter took of what was true in him–healing–and gave it. Jesus gave of what was true about Himself, and He gave it to you. Healing is freely yours and freely yours to give. It's part of your identity.

My story about the birth of our second child, Olivia, all started with my platelets being so dangerously low that I had to deliver her immediately, even though it was prior to 38 weeks. The danger of my platelets being low again and bleeding to death in any subsequent pregnancy were high.  My doctor told me that some women's platelet levels drop significantly in the third trimester, and I was one of them. And because my usual platelet levels even when I wasn't pregnant were on the low end, this would make pregnancy and childbirth very dangerous for me and the baby. Because of this, my husband and I decided that we would not try for a third child like we had planned.

About six years later, we had the incredible surprise that I was pregnant again! Even though I was so excited for our new baby, one of my first thoughts was, What are we going to do about my platelets?

There was a difference with this pregnancy, though. This time, I knew my identity. I knew that healing was true of me, because it's true of Jesus. God had given me the revelations of Jesus in the temple and how Jesus never asked God to heal anyone. He had shown me how Peter and Paul would freely give of the healing that had been given to them. And I knew the story of my friend, Lindsay, who just like Jesus, told what didn't belong to leave, and it did.

This time, I remembered how much I look like Jesus.

I literally stood and pointed my finger and said, "Platelets, you will not drop to a dangerous level in my third trimester. You will stay at a high count the entire pregnancy and delivery." And that was it. That was all I said. And I never said anything contrary to that.

We were living in a different state than where our older girls were born, so I had a new OB for this pregnancy. Given my medical history, my new doctor would check my platelets on a regular basis all throughout my pregnancy. Her plan was to monitor them and, if they dropped too low, she would induce me as early as possible and still be safe for the baby.

To give some context, a normal range for blood platelets is anywhere between 150,000 to 450,000 platelets per microliter of blood. Mine were are at 150,000 to begin with and dropped to 14,000 when I gave birth to our second daughter. My doctor felt that as long as my count stayed above 80,000, we could hold out for me to go into labor on my own.

As the weeks and months went by, my platelets stayed in a healthy range, but given what had happened with my previous pregnancy, my doctor started testing for my count even more often. When we got to 39 weeks, my doctor decided that the baby had gotten to a size and weight that could make delivery dangerous for the baby if we let her stay in for too long, so

The health and
wholeness of the body
of Christ is your health.
*It's who He is, and it's
who you are.*

she decided to induce me. After hours of labor, the baby wasn't budging. The baby had gotten into a part of the birth canal where, if she stayed for too long, it could cause complications for her. So, the doctor told me we had to have an emergency c-section, and they rushed me to the operating room. Throughout the labor she had been continually checking my platelet count. I think the only thing more dangerous than giving birth with low blood platelets is having surgery with low platelets! The first time my platelets dropped I couldn't even have the needle from an epidural let alone a surgery that made an opening large enough for a baby to pass through. If I ever needed my platelet count high, it would be for a c-section. And this time, the final count right before surgery was not just out of the critical zone, it was at 260,000! Higher than I had ever tested even when I wasn't pregnant! I gave birth to Evre in perfect health!

Healing and wholeness are yours, too! Everything about you looks like Jesus, and this is your moment to look up and see the health and healing of Jesus. This is your moment to see the passion Jesus has for your healing and the wholeness of your body. As Paul wrote, "Don't you realize that all of you together are the temple of God and that the Spirit of God lives in you? God will destroy anyone who destroys this temple. For God's temple is holy, and you are that temple." 1 Corinthians 3:16-17 (NLT)

This is the moment that you awaken to who you are and all that you have. Your life is Christ's Life. Your health is Christ's health. Your body was passionately rescued. The health and wholeness of the body of Christ is your health. It's who He is, and it's who you are.

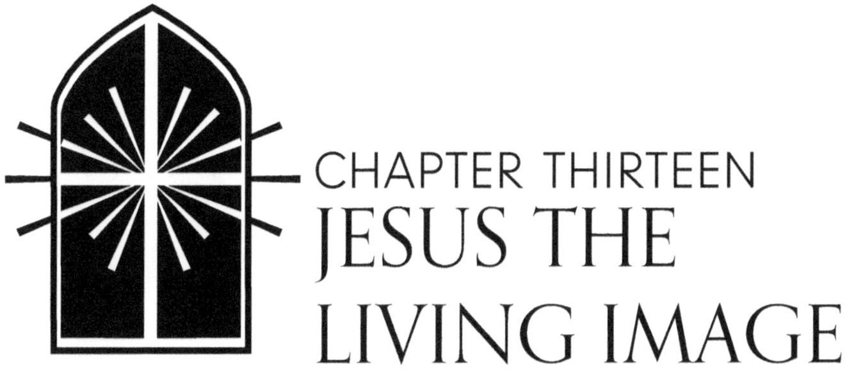

# CHAPTER THIRTEEN
# JESUS THE LIVING IMAGE

This gospel unveils a continual revelation of God's righteousness—a perfect righteousness given to us when we believe. And it moves us from receiving life through faith, to the power of living by faith. This is what the Scripture means when it says: "We are right with God through life-giving faith!" Romans 1:17 (TPT)

In the parable of the prodigal son, Jesus gives us incredible insight into the mind of a believer. This story tells of a wayward son and speaks beautifully to the truth that, originally, the younger son of the father began in his father's home as part of his family, then made the choice to leave. This portrait of redemption mirrors our story. Yet, that's not the story that most compels me about Jesus' parable. The character that captivates me is the older brother.

The father's older son remained in his father's house. He never turned from his father or his father's business. He was faithful and diligent. But, he lacked one thing. And that was his awareness of his identity. And without that understanding, he lived within a paradigm that limited him.

When the sorrowful, younger son returned, his father brought out all of his best to celebrate his return. The ring, the robe, the feast, and the father's embrace communicated more than just a celebration. The father was telling his son his identity.

"Turning to his servants, the father said, 'Quick, bring me the best robe, my very own robe, and I will place it on his shoulders. Bring the ring, the seal of sonship, and I will put it on his finger. And bring out the best shoes you can find for my son. For this beloved son of mine was once dead, but now he's alive again. Once he was lost, but now he is found!' And everyone celebrated with overflowing joy." Luke 15:22, 24 (TPT)

These gifts were not meant to exclude the older brother. In fact, these gifts communicated the identity of the older brother as well. But, his misunderstanding of his place in their family turned a wealthy, loved man into a servant in his own home.

> Now, the older son was out working in the field when his brother returned, and as he approached the house he heard the music of celebration and dancing. So, he called over one of the servants and asked, "What's going on?" The servant replied, "It's your younger brother. He's returned home and your father is throwing a party to celebrate his homecoming." The older son became angry and refused to go in and celebrate. So, his father came out and pleaded with him, "Come and enjoy the feast with us." The son said, "Father, listen! How many years have I been working like a slave for you, performing every duty you've asked as a faithful son? And I've never once disobeyed you. But you've never thrown a party for me because of my faithfulness. Never once have you even given me a goat that I could feast on and celebrate with my friends like he's doing now. But look at this son of yours! He comes back after wasting your wealth on prostitutes and reckless living, and here you are throwing a great feast to celebrate—for him!" The father said, **"My son, you are always with me by my side. Everything I have is yours to enjoy**. It's only right to celebrate like this and be overjoyed, because this brother of yours was once dead." Luke 15:25-32 (TPT)

The older son lived his life as if his own merit, and his own striving, would gain him the inheritance that was already his. It was his, not because of anything he could have achieved, but because he was his father's son. This was his birthright. Who he was determined what he had, even if he didn't realize it. He had his father's presence, and all that the father had was his because of the blood that they shared. Yet, he lived as if he was a slave.

How have we, who have been made joint heirs with Christ and who are seated with Him, confined ourselves to this same paradigm as the older brother? What have we believed we had to earn? What did we think belonged to us only on the other side of eternity that is actually already ours here and now?

Some of us have found ourselves in a constant cycle of striving to work for what Jesus has already secured for you.  What have we believed about ourselves to justify this idea? What have we believed about God that caused us to see him as distant? What have we believed about the Father that told us we had to earn our place and our inheritance in His family? Only One could have earned this, yet He was the only One who righteously had it all before time began. The Righteous Heir gave you His righteousness. He gave you His name. The ring of sonship in the parable represented a seal of identity.

> For all the promises of God find their Yes in him. That is why it is through him that we utter our Amen to God for his glory. And it is God who establishes us with you in Christ, and has anointed us, and who has also put his seal on us and given us his Spirit in our hearts as a guarantee. 2 Corinthians 1:20-22 (ESV)

Jesus takes us from receiving His salvation to living His salvation. Living in our new identity is living in Christ. So many believers spend their lives trying to receive what they already have. For too long, the children of God have lived in a way that confined them as slaves instead of sons, exactly like the older brother in the parable.

These verses from the Bible about being joint heirs with Christ and being made the righteousness of God are not figurative language. The sacrifice that Jesus made for you to be with Him, as He is with the Father, is not figurative. His life, His death, and His resurrection were not figurative. His life is ours.

When we look at Jesus, it's as if we are looking in a mirror. His light reflects onto us as we reflect His likeness.

> But when the fullness of time had come, God sent forth his Son, born of woman, born under the law, to redeem those who were under the law, so that we might receive adoption as sons. And because you are sons, God has sent the Spirit of his Son into our hearts, crying, "Abba! Father!" So you are no longer a slave, but a son, and if a son, then an heir through God. Galatians 4:4-7 (ESV)

Even in our crying out, Abba Father, His Spirit is declaring that if we have the right to call Him Father, then we are His children. The only way to find your identity is to look to Jesus. When you come to the end of yourself, you find the beginning of Him. You find your beginning.

> Throughout our history God has spoken to our ancestors by his prophets in many different ways. The revelation he gave them was only a fragment at a time, building one truth upon another. But to us living in these last days, God now speaks to us openly in the language of a Son, the appointed Heir of everything, for through him God created the panorama of all things and all time. Hebrews 1:1-2 (TPT)

God speaks to us in the language of a Son. Jesus, the Word, is the language we know innately because it is this language by which our existence is coded.

Ryan's career has led him to meet many fascinating people who live and work in different spheres of influence and study than most people. Ryan would come home from meeting with a Quantum Physicist and talk to me about all of the latest discoveries and mysteries in Quantum Mechanics that they discussed. Each new thing I would hear, I had biblical context for. What seemed to be a study far beyond anything that I had ever learned simultaneously seemed as if I already knew. These were revelations that God had given me about Him, and us. Quantum was discovering truth through science, but it has been in the Bible all along.

Quantum Physics is arguably the most accurate form of science and yet it is held as theory with great wonder surrounding it. The greatest mystery of quantum is referred to as the measurement problem. Quantum is known as the hidden realm. It's a realm they know exists, but have no known tools or methods to measure it. The closest form they can give this unknown reality is that the quantum realm is made of waves. Not literal waves, as we know them in water or sound, but abstract waves. It depicts a world of highly accurate probability and yet immeasurability at the same time.

Quantum Physics has discovered that the entire universe, and all creation including humanity, is held together by this hidden realm. What we know to be the smallest particles of matter that make up all of existence, are made of quantum waves that have moved past the barrier from the unseen world and into the seen. These abstract waves, once past the barrier, become seen and known as particles. The atoms and all that is within each atom to form you and all creation are the seen form of the unseen. Where these particles end, another dimension begins, far greater than the world we have measured. Quantum has found a window into a world that is more complex than the most intricate systems on earth.

At this point in history, all that science can see is the existence of this hidden realm but they cannot explain it. Many people have falsely attributed Quantum to spirit or the kingdom of heaven. To be clear, Quantum is not either of those. Quantum is another parable by God to reveal Jesus. God has used parables throughout the earth since the beginning of time to reveal Jesus just as Jesus used parables to explain the Kingdom of God. In His goodness, God has given us parables that speak to the culture and technology of each era as a way to know Him better. Jesus used the parables of planting, fishing, masters and servants, and other metaphors that were relevant in that time to the people of that day. In today's culture, the idea of Quantum physics and the ability to observe it are relevant and pique interest. The newness of this science and the mystery that surrounds it can seem mystical to people. But, the reality is that the science of Quantum is no more mystical than the science that taught us how an acorn can fall from a tree, go into the ground, and produce another tree. It is no more mystical that the stars in the sky. They point to Jesus.

> God's splendor is a tale that is told; his testament is
> written in the stars. Space itself speaks his story every day

through the marvels of the heavens. His truth is on tour
in the starry vault of the sky, showing his skill in creation's
craftsmanship. Psalms 19:1 (TPT)

Quantum is simply explained as the part of physics that describes the
smallest particles. Where we once thought all existence ended within
ourselves at our smallest particles of matter, we now see that each particle,
the smallest piece of our matter, ends at this barrier. And yet, this barrier
is just the beginning. Where we thought we ended, we were only just
beginning. There is a way, a barrier, that has been torn open to peer into a
reality far greater than what we knew to be all there was. The parallel of this
discovery to the revelation of Jesus is incredible. There is so much more to
see looking into the mirror as we see Jesus face to face. We cannot measure
with creation the Creator. But, creation can be measured in Him.

The Tower of Babel lacked the measurement it needed to reach heaven
because their unified language was not the right language. There was only
one language that would translate all of creation into the unseen realm.

> Throughout our history God has spoken to our ancestors
> by his prophets in many different ways. The revelation he
> gave them was only a fragment at a time, building one
> truth upon another. **But to us living in these last days,
> God now speaks to us openly in the language of a Son,**
> the appointed Heir of everything, for through him God
> created the panorama of all things and all time. **The Son
> is the dazzling radiance of God's splendor, the exact
> expression of God's true nature–his mirror image!** He
> holds the universe together and expands it by the mighty
> power of his spoken word. He accomplished for us the
> complete cleansing of sins, and then took his seat on
> the highest throne at the right hand of the majestic One.
> Hebrews 1:1-3 (TPT)

There was a veil that had to be torn - a barrier that had to be passed - to get
to the Father. Jesus is the measurement by which all creation is redeemed.
Jesus is the Language by which we have communion with the Father. He
is the One whose death on the cross tore the veil that separated humanity

There was a veil that had
to be torn - a barrier that
had to be passed - to get
to the Father. Jesus is the
measurement by which all
creation is redeemed. Jesus
is the *Language by which we
have communion
with the Father.*

from the Presence of God. Science is reaching out to find our origins, to find what holds us all together. And now, because Jesus left the unseen to be seen in our place, we can begin to look and see the greater reality of the kingdom of heaven. God is not holding us back; He's drawing us in to see Him. And to see ourselves in the Son.

Humanity apart from God will search for an identity that is limited to themselves. 2 Corinthians 10:12 says, "They compare themselves to one another and make up their own standards to measure themselves by, and then they judge themselves by their own standards, What self-delusion!" (TPT) Without Christ, if you look to find your identity within yourself, you will come to that place where you end and there will be nowhere else to go. You will find that you are incomplete. And yet, even in this, God is still speaking His love for you because that ache in you that longs to know your identity is placed there by God to lead you to Jesus.

> Christ's resurrection is your resurrection too. This is why we are to yearn for all that is above, for that's where Christ sits enthroned at the place of all power, honor, and authority! Yes, feast on all the treasures of the heavenly realm and fill your thoughts with heavenly realities, and not with the distractions of the natural realm. **Your crucifixion with Christ has severed the tie to this life, and now your true life is hidden away in God in Christ. And as Christ himself is seen for who he really is, who you really are will also be revealed, for you are now one with him in his glory!** Colossians 3:1-4 (TPT)

Superposition is a physical phenomenon that illuminates quantum in our physical realm. To put it in its most basic terms, it is the discovery that something can be in two places at once. This modern-day marvel is a beautiful picture of our union with Jesus. You are both here on earth and, simultaneously, seated with Christ in heaven. As Jesus is fully God and fully Man, you have been translated into the realm where your spirit is joined to the Spirit of God. Here on earth as it is in heaven. Where you thought you ended, you were only just beginning.

The body of Jesus was unrecognizable at his death. His flesh torn and His body broken. They laid the Man they thought was immortal in the tomb. The One they believed would reign as King laid dead in the grave. The death on a wooden cross, cursed and shamed, broke every perception the followers of Jesus had of the One they thought to be their Savior. And even in this we see the truth: What they thought was the end, was actually only the beginning. His death was just the beginning of His resurrection. Your death being crucified with Christ, was just the beginning of your salvation. Your identity apart from Jesus ended, and at that point, your identity began. Where you end, He begins.

> In the very beginning the Living Expression was already there. And the Living Expression was with God, yet fully God. They were together—face-to-face, in the very beginning. And through his creative inspiration this Living Expression made all things, for nothing has existence apart from him! Life came into being because of him, for his life is light for all humanity. John 1:1-4 (TPT)

About ten years ago, I had an encounter with Jesus that forever changed how I saw Him, and in turn, how I saw myself. I was standing with my hands lifted to about my waist in a moment of worship and prayer, and Jesus gave me a picture of Him standing in front of me. I had always pictured that, as a believer, Jesus was in me. For example, if I was facing east, He was facing east. If I used my right hand, I was moving the right hand of Jesus. This was all figurative in my perspective, but the curious thing is that I never pictured Him in front of me. If anything, I unwittingly pictured Him as if I couldn't see Him with my own eyes if He was standing inside of me.

But in this moment, Jesus stood before me. He had His left hand under my right, and His right under my left, holding my hands up with the palms of His. While it's true that we are made of Him, this is not the end, it's only the beginning. As He has rolled out revelation upon revelation over the years of this moment with Him, I've seen new dimensions of the reality of identity.

If you were looking in a mirror, and moved your right hand, your mirror image would look like it was waving its left hand. This is reflection. When we take a selfie on our phones, our image is reflected so that if your image on the screen were an actual physical being, when your reflection would mimic

—————

A mirror image creates a
completion. A full circle.
*Where one ends, the other
begins.* It forms a loop
that is infinite and yet
complete in union.

—————

your movements, then it would be using the opposite side of yours to reflect your image.

A mirror image creates a completion. A full circle. Where one ends, the other begins. It forms a loop that is infinite and yet complete in union. This entanglement brings what would have been separate, into one. Jesus, who has gone ahead of us in every way, first lived this way for us to follow. He took upon Himself our separation on the cross, but He lived a life before that on earth in a complete union with the Father that we could not have without Him. As Colossians 1:15 tells us, "Christ is the visible image of the invisible God." (NLT) And He will always be the perfect image of the Father for all eternity. The Bible also speaks of you. It speaks of those who become the Children of God. Ephesians 6:2 (AMP) reveals, "And He raised us up together with Him [when we believed], and seated us with Him in the heavenly places, [because we are] in Christ Jesus,"

Our bodies are on this earth, but our spirits, our truest selves, are already seated in heaven. With that truth in mind, we will look at 1 Corinthians 15:49, "Just as we have borrne the image of the earthly [the man from dust], we will also bear the image of the heavenly [the Man of heaven]."

You bear the image of Jesus. You are His mirror image.

Quantum physics has found a parallel that is being used by God to draw humanity into the revelation of Christ. Entanglement is the word used to describe the phenomena of two waves becoming one and the space between them becomes irrelevant. As one is, so the other is. When two are entangled, if one spins to the right, the other will spin to the left. They are one, and a mirror image of each other. When entanglement happens, there is something, still unknown to physicists, that links the two together. Yet, we know the One who brought God and Man together again. The One who is God and Man. He is the One who holds us all together. This scientific mystery is a mirror image of the mystery of Christ and His Church. It's the miracle of Resurrection Life. At the moment of salvation, Jesus breathed His Spirit into you, to entangle you to Him for all eternity.

> But the moment one turns to the Lord with an open
> heart, the veil is lifted and they see. Now, the "Lord" I'm
> referring to is the Holy Spirit, and wherever he is Lord,

You bear the image
of Jesus. You are *His*

*mirror image.*

there is freedom. We can all draw close to him with the veil
removed from our faces. And with no veil we all become
like mirrors who brightly reflect the glory of the Lord
Jesus. We are being transfigured into his very image as we
move from one brighter level of glory to another. And this
glorious transfiguration comes from the Lord, who is the
Spirit. 2 Corinthians 3:18 (TPT)

Jesus is drawing you into a continual and eternal revelation of who He is. And
the more you see Jesus for who He is, the more you will reflect His image as
the light of His face shines on you.

I can think of no better way to bring this book to a close than with the words
of John. He knew Jesus with an intimacy that beckons us into a life with Jesus
marked by His Presence and love. John wrote of knowing Jesus as the Living
Expression who made all things, and in whom all things exist. The beginning
and the End. The Creator who  became creation. The last book of the Bible is
a revelation of the identity of Jesus. John, the author of Revelation, is the one
Jesus entrusted with the book designed to reveal Himself. He pens, in 1 John
4:17 (TPT), the revelation of your identity as well. Because you will never find
your identity in yourself. And your identity is not even the identity that you
are meant to seek out. You are meant to seek out and find the identity of
Jesus by looking at Him, and in Him, you are found.

*"because all that Jesus now is, so are we in this world."*

Finding your identity has never been the goal or prize. Rather, the identity of
Jesus and His fullness is our inheritance to discover throughout eternity. May
this moment be just the beginning of a lifetime of revelations of Jesus. And
as the light of His face shines on you may you reflect His glory. You are His
mirror image.

———

Jesus is drawing you into a continual and eternal revelation of who He is. And the more you see Jesus for who He is, *the more you will reflect His image* as the light of His face shines on you.

———

# AN INVITATION

The one who is the true light, who gives light to everyone, was coming into the world. He came into the very world he created, but the world didn't recognize him. He came to his own people, and even they rejected him. But to all who believed him and accepted him, he gave the right to become children of God. John 1:9-12 ( NLT)

My heart for you is that this book would invite you into a life with Jesus that He died for you to live. For some, that will mean going from glory to glory by moving deeper into the life that began when Jesus breathed His breath of Life and Spirit into their spirits at their moment of rebirth into the family of God. For others, this will be an invitation to die. To be crucified with Christ so that His resurrection would be theirs. And, for some, they will come to the end of themselves, to find their beginning in Him. Jesus is standing in front of you. Will you look up? Will you accept His invitation to become one with Him?

And what is God's "living message"? It is the revelation of faith for salvation, which is the message that we preach. For if you publicly declare with your mouth that Jesus is Lord and believe in your heart that God raised him from the dead, you will experience salvation. The heart that believes in him receives the gift of the righteousness of God—and then the mouth confesses, resulting in salvation. For the Scriptures encourage us with these words: "Everyone who believes in him will never be disappointed." Romans 10:9-11 (TPT)

# ABOUT THE AUTHOR

Briana Collins has over 25 years of ministry experience. She has served the local church as a pastor, worship leader, and counselor. Most recently, Briana has been engaged in building up the global church as a speaker and author. Briana is married to her husband, Ryan, and they have three brilliant daughters.

www.ingramcontent.com/pod-product-compliance
Lightning Source LLC
Chambersburg PA
CBHW041311120726
48005CB00014B/1958